The Aston Martin and Lagonda
Volume 1: Six-cylinder DB models

The Aston Martin and Lagonda
Vol 1: Six-cylinder DB models

A collector's guide
by Andrew Whyte

MOTOR RACING PUBLICATIONS LTD
Unit 6, The Pilton Estate, 46 Pitlake, Croydon CR0 3RY, England

ISBN 0 900549 83 1
First published 1984
Second Edition 1988

Photosetting by Zee Creative Ltd, London SW16
Printed in Great Britain by Adlard & Son Ltd, The Garden City Press
Letchworth, Hertfordshire SG6 1JS

Contents

Introduction and acknowledgements

Although they were conceived in entirely different ways, the Aston Martin and Lagonda marques have many things in common, and their paths crossed long before they came together permanently.

Their founders competed with the cars they made in sporting events, and when the two marques became established names on the scene at Brooklands and Le Mans they were rivals for British prestige in international events. To buy one was not merely to demonstrate wealth and taste, but also to show an appreciation of British engineering at its specialized best. That is a tradition which can truly be claimed to continue today — a tradition which has kept the marques alive through many changes of fortune and ownership.

Both achieved the goal of winning the great Le Mans 24-hour race. Lagonda did it, in 1935, at a time when it could not capitalize on the success, due to the appointment of a Receiver shortly beforehand. The story of how Aston Martin came to the chequered flag in the French classic (24 *years* later!) is one of fulfilment, for it opened the way to Britain's only victory to date in the World Sports Car Championship.

It is not unnatural that the series-production cars, as well as the competition models, should be thoroughly bespoke in nature. The collector, seeking the car of his preference, may well find some aspect different from what he expected. This is not necessarily the result of a less-than-thorough restoration. Specialist manufacturers could, and did, make cars for individuals, and to individual specifications; they could also change the specification at will. I think it is probably reasonable to say that no two Aston Martins (and, maybe, Lagondas) were ever *exactly* alike in every detail. It is therefore impossible to include in a book of this size a definitive list of all updating modifications.

What I have tried to do is clarify the relationships between the six-cylinder models built since (Sir) David Brown brought Aston Martin and Lagonda together, thereby undoubtedly saving them from the fate which they have continually glimpsed. I have also tried to highlight the tricky path trodden between the costly joys and miseries of motor racing and the commercial needs of car-making for an inconsistently enthusiastic public.

More important to the collector, however, are the pointers to the help and advice needed by anyone new to ownership or contemplating it. There *are* people who run Aston Martins and Lagondas of the 'Fifties and 'Sixties regularly on the road without a care — but it is unusual. Generally, the need to find a kindred spirit is felt from the start. Fortunately — for the writer as well as the owner — the Aston Martins and Lagondas of the past live today in a fairly tight community of knowledge and experience.

I should like to thank in particular the many people of the marque clubs who have helped and advised me while compiling this book. I am sure they will be just as helpful to any new owner who turns to them. For their co-operation on interpreting vehicle identity and on photography I am especially grateful to Ivan and Richard Forshaw and to Jack and Simon Moss — all famed for their special knowledge. My appreciation is also due to those who allowed their cars to be photographed, and to the publishers of both *Motor* and *Autocar* for permission to reprint pictures from their archives. Particular thanks, too, to Alan Archer of the AMOC for his invaluable co-operation.

Many people who worked under Sir David Brown and John Wyer have helped me to imagine what it was like, and here I must single out Harold Beach and Frank Feeley — two of the most significant names in this story — for the conversations we had. Finally, at Newport Pagnell itself, no-one could have been more helpful than Roger Stowers in putting me on the right track for both the words *and* the pictures.

The future of the two marques may be as uncertain as it has ever been; the cars may not be entirely practical, but they have retained their individuality and magnetic charm. Even if some corners have to be cut in achieving it (for example, the use of proprietary engines), the survival of the charismatic Aston Martin and Lagonda marques still seems feasible.

The enthusiasm for the cars covered by this book ensures that there will always be plenty of 'DBs' being enjoyed on the road or in historic racing, upholding a great tradition. Long may this be the case.

February 1984   ANDREW WHYTE

Sir David Brown, whose acquisition of Aston Martin and Lagonda soon after the Second World War was to lead to the production and sporting success of so many fine cars.

John Wyer, whose team management and then technical direction of Aston Martin Lagonda did so much to enhance the reputation of the company, both on the race track and in the high-performance luxury car market.

CHAPTER 1

Dual heritage

Aston Martin and Lagonda before David Brown

It was Allard enthusiast Dermot Johnston of the Ulster Automobile Club who suggested puckishly in the winter of 1950-51 that, as no DB2s had yet been delivered to private owners, Aston Martin were not really in business to sell cars, but were merely racing for fun. He made this remark while thanking John Wyer for a talk he had given.

Wyer had just completed his first season as Team Manager for David Brown, who had recently added Aston Martin and Lagonda to his group of companies. Efforts to refute the idea were, it was said, deafened by the enthusiastic applause for Wyer's after-dinner speech.

Only a few weeks earlier, most of those present would have seen the works Aston Martins following-up an excellent Le Mans result with a class 1-2-3 in the first Tourist Trophy to be held on Ulster's narrow, abrasive and tricky new Dundrod circuit — one of the few true road courses upon which cars have ever been allowed to race in the UK.

Johnston's mischievous suggestion was half-right, though, for Wyer had had a difficult start diplomatically. Naturally, one of his first jobs at Aston Martin had been driver selection, and almost before his feet were under the table at Feltham his boss had told him that *he*, David Brown, wanted to be a team driver at Le Mans! Fortunately, Stanley Barnes, of the Royal Automobile Club — who handled certain aspects of the British Le Mans entries — put two-and-two together and told Wyer what he knew already. It was not that Brown was too old (though he *was* in his middle forties); he just did not have the experience to take part in the world's most famous motor race. Armed with the authority of the RAC, Wyer was able (without jeopardizing his own new job,

to which he was looking forward so much) to persuade Brown not to go motor racing after all.

The tremendous success of six-cylinder Aston Martin cars in certain motor races over the next decade was largely attributable to Wyer's management. It is fair to say that bad luck played a big part in Aston Martin's Le Mans involvement during their period of greatest activity. It was always David Brown's ambition that one of his cars would win Le Mans outright, but it was not until 1959 that an Aston Martin finally did it, and by that time, the steam had gone out of the sports car racing effort, though Brown did still have ambitions on the Grand Prix front. However, that almost unexpected 1959 Le Mans victory suddenly put Aston Martin in a position to become Britain's first World Sports Car Champions, a task which they completed by winning the TT again.

In reaching their pinnacle, the 1959 team cars were already obsolescent. All the work of a decade had nevertheless come together just before it was too late. There have been many outstanding Aston Martin achievements since then, but that year stands out from all others as the year of glory and of personal triumph for Brown who, 12 years earlier, had bought Aston Martin — as a business venture, yes; but also, as he admitted later, because he thought it would be . . . (his word) fun.

Soon afterwards, David Brown had acquired Lagonda as well even if, at first, the Lagonda company had not interested him. Although he now owned Aston Martin, he was not collecting names. Then W.O. Bentley showed him a new engine, which made him change his mind, for he felt that it was just what Aston Martin needed.

Lagonda — the early years

The story of Lagonda began considerably earlier than that of Aston Martin. To ears used to the English language, Lagonda could sound more like the name of an Italian restaurant than that of one of Britain's proudest motor cars. It is the sort of name that begs the question: Why?

When people of different nations meet, they play havoc with one another's languages. French-speaking traders probably originated the word now spelt Lagonda as they copied the sound of the name Shawnee Indians gave to a meandering, backwater stream which twisted 'like the horns of a buck' through Ohio, one of the new United States of North America. Lagonda, or Bucks Horn Creek, was later anglicized to Buck Creek; the early settlement of Lagonda is now swallowed up by industrial Springfield, once a neighbouring village.

The early white settlers included the Methodist Gunn family, and in 1859 Wilbur Adams Gunn was born into it. Several years earlier Isaac Singer, of Boston, had invented his sewing machine. His company developed on both sides of the Atlantic, and in due course Gunn became a trainee, later to return to Springfield, Ohio. There he married in 1885, and worked as a sewing machine inspector.

The marriage lasted 14 years, but Gunn emigrated to Britain sometime during that period — alone. Singer had UK connections from the outset, but that fact is not necessarily a related one. Much of Gunn's life is shrouded in mystery. It can be stated, however, that he settled on the Surrey side of the Thames at Staines before the turn of the century. There he made motor bicycles with the name Lagonda for, presumably, nostalgic reasons.

From 1904, there were tricycles and tricars, including a number for carrying the Royal Mail. A century earlier, his ancestor Horace Gunn had been the first regular deliverer of mail to the Lagonda and Springfield localities by river, and so it is interesting to note that Wilbur Gunn and his first UK assistant, Alfred Cranmer, are thought to have done some boatbuilding, too.

All the indications are that the Lagonda factory, which had started in the existing outbuildings of his home, cannot have been Gunn's only business interest, for production was sporadic to say the least. In 1905, he made best performance in the MCC London-to-Edinburgh Trial, the first true publicity for Lagonda as a marque. From 1907, the company was in the hands of the receiver, and early in 1910 it was sold — apparently to Gunn, whose work in developing the first Lagonda car during that period must have impressed those handling his affairs.

The development was quick for, with his right-hand man Bert Hammond, Gunn won the Russian reliability trial of 1910 in one of his own cars. The trial itself was very long, looping from St Petersburg southwards through White Russia and the Ukraine before turning north again to Moscow. It was, however, very boring and it produced no clear winner. For reasons unknown, Gunn was the only entrant to take up the tie-deciding challenge — a race back to St Petersburg by the direct route, which he and Hammond completed in less than 12 hours. The Tsar himself was photographed making presentations to Gunn, and for the next few years Russia was Lagonda's main export market.

In 1913, the company was reconstituted from Lagonda Motor Company to Lagonda Ltd and Gunn introduced his small, modern, unit-construction 11.1hp model. During the Great War, the Lagonda machine shop was put to full use making precision components for shells. Ill-health was dogging Gunn by now, and although he won another gold medal in the revived London-to-Edinburgh Trial of 1920, he died before the year was out, still an enigma, but undoubtedly a pioneering motor car manufacturer of stature.

From 1913, Gunn had three co-directors to help keep the company going financially and, after his death, the sporting image was maintained. In 1921, several light car speed records were broken by Lagonda at Brooklands, only to be beaten by Aston Martin the following week. As time went on, Lagondas usually ran in a engine capacity class above that of the Aston Martins, but the parallels continued.

Both marques, for example, first ran at Le Mans in 1928, and both reached their peak in 1935 — Lagonda winning outright and Aston Martin coming third and winning the Rudge-Whitworth Cup for the second year running. Bertie Kensington-Moir, an early Aston Martin advocate and the man who had taken away the record from Lagonda at Brooklands, took some time off from Bentleys in the late 'Twenties to look after Lagonda's racing affairs. The biggest successes, however, came with the help of Arthur Fox and Robert Nicholl, whose establishment at Tolworth, Surrey, was also deeply involved in the preparation of English Talbots for racing and rallying.

It was a Fox and Nicholl entry at that great Le Mans race of 1935 which took Lagonda to its competition peak, when the 4½-litre Meadows-engined M45 Rapide of John Hindmarsh and Luis Fontes (an Englishman, though his name was Spanish) ended four years of Alfa Romeo rule at Le Mans. The works Alfa Romeos retired, as did the leading French opposition, and the British crew scored a narrow victory over the 2.3-litre Alfa of Frenchmen Louis Heldé and veteran Henri Stoffel. (The latter was one of Le Mans' 'bridesmaids', for he was third on two occasions and runner-up three times, getting very close to winning, but never quite doing so.) Third was the 1½-litre Aston Martin of Charles Brackenbury and Charles Martin, giving

A typically elegant 'Silent Travel' Lagonda pillarless saloon from the early 'Thirties. However, the company was approaching one of its financial crises, and by 1935 it had been wound up and restarted again.

The harmonious curves of the 1938 V12 drophead coupe would remain a Lagonda characteristic after the war. Ace wheel discs were optional, and welcomed by Meccano, who were thus able to make a fine Dinky model of this beautiful car with its twin covered side-mounted spare wheels.

Feltham *its* best prewar result.

This success could not help Lagonda out of the financial trouble which caught up with it again that year. The products may have looked like becoming natural successors to the vintage Bentleys, but Alan Good oversaw a complete change of direction for the Staines company, and it was a change for the better, only to be cut short by the intervention of war.

His own failed company absorbed by Rolls-Royce, Walter Owen Bentley was brought in (with Richard Watney as Managing Director) to take responsibility for Lagonda design.

First of all, Bentley 'civilized' the big six-cylinder Lagonda, giving it a synchromesh gearbox and moving the engine back in the chassis. Bentley also made its Meadows engine breathe and rev more freely, but it was his V12 power unit — also a '4½' — which pitched Lagonda into the top luxury bracket. The completely new engine had a relatively short stroke and one camshaft for each bank of cylinders. A 'Bentley' feature of the new car's chassis was its cruciform central structure. Independent front suspension was by torsion bars, and this magnificent machine, clothed in Lagonda or proprietary

By 1937, W.O. Bentley's influence was much in evidence, this four-door saloon revealing an elegance which even cars bearing his own name would do well to match. Both six-cylinder and V12-engined cars were produced at this time on chassis of slightly differing lengths.

coachwork of unusual elegance, offered motoring in the grand style, making it a genuine alternative to the 'Best Car in the World' which, in V12 Phantom III form, was typically enormous, but of uncertain reliability. With the royal Daimler marque appearing to go slightly down-market, the late 'Thirties could have led Lagonda to greater things. The sporting heritage was well-maintained during this period and a particularly workmanlike performance was put in by two lightened and tuned V12-engined cars at Le Mans in 1939, when their third and fourth places were due more to strict team discipline than to lack

of pace.

Alan Good and his brother Magnus had come from Ireland where their father had given each of them a certain sum, believed to be £1,000, to make their way in the world. It is thought that Good began his business career in wholesale meat marketing at Smithfield, but he moved on to Lincoln's Inn to become a City solicitor or, as some remarked, a 'city slicker'. He has even been described as a mountebank.

Acquisition of one firm can lead to the opportunity to borrow in order to purchase others. Alan Good was involved in several

13

famous diesel engine companies, such as Mirrlees and Petter; but he failed to gain Gardner and Perkins, without which monopoly would be impossible. His biggest coup was Brush, of Loughborough, whose involvement in the rail and road transport industries was considerable.

Such organizations were much more in Good's spheres of interest by the end of the Second World War, though he *had* competed in rallies with his Lagondas, had instigated the 1939 V12 Le Mans entries, and had played his part in influencing design, too. Wartime for Lagonda meant munitions work once again, although towards the end of it William Watson (subsequently of Invicta Black Prince fame) was able to devote his time to postwar Lagonda car design. Donald Bastow, *en route* from Rolls-Royce to Jowett, also helped.

Watson also had a lot to do with the final design of the twin-overhead-camshaft six-cylinder engine which is attributed to W.O. Bentley. This project began as the four, six and eight-cylinder LB4, LB6 and LB8. In the end, only the LB6 progressed, and through it came the permanent link with Aston Martin. David Brown bought the company and W.O. Bentley went into virtual retirement, forming a design consultancy in Weybridge, where he was joined by several Lagonda folk, including Donald Bastow. Managing Director Dick Watney returned to his old firm, the Rootes Group, and died in a road accident. Alan Good hung on to the Wilbur Gunn home-cum-factory site in Staines, and put Petters Ltd into it, having sold David Brown the goodwill, some parts and prototypes *and*, of course, that variation of an old American Indian name — Lagonda.

Aston Martin — the early years

The first Aston Martin car did not make its presence felt until motoring and the motor car were everyday things. Indeed, it did not appear as a named marque until after the Great War.

Earlier, an English gentleman called Lionel Martin had been driving modified Singers in competitions, and it might be argued that the now-illustrious title 'Aston Martin' is something of a misnomer, for two reasons. The first is that, on the occasion which prompted it, Martin was not driving a car made by him or his engineer-partner Robert Bamford. The second reason is that his 'Aston' performance was not really a winning one.

It was in 1913 that Lionel Martin first figured in the results of the short-distance speed events which — apart from Brooklands — were the nearest thing to road-racing mainland Britain could offer. That June, at the South Harting hill-climb, not far from Goodwood in Sussex, Archie Nash (later called Frazer-Nash) won the 1,100cc four-wheeler class driving one of the GN cyclecars which he and his partner Ron Godfrey had been building since 1910. In second place, but considerably slower, was Lionel Martin's Singer — a more modern design, with four-cylinder side-valve 1,100cc engine and rear axle-mounted gearbox, and lightened just enough to run in the lightweight class occupied by cyclecars.

It was from the village of Aston Clinton, near Aylesbury (or rather the hill leading from it up into the Chilterns) that the Aston Martin ultimately got its name. Despite its lightness, Martin's 10hp Singer simply could not approach the power-to-weight ratio of the 12hp V-twin Buckingham driven by its constructor in the May 1914 event. The Buckingham weighed less than 7cwt and beat the Singer by 3.8 seconds; nevertheless, the handicap formula employed by the Hertfordshire County Automobile Club that day gave Martin the prize which would lead him to add the name of the location to his own.

Probably Lionel Martin's finest performance of the year came soon afterwards, just before motor sports came to an end for the duration. On the last weekend of June, the timed climb of the Caerphilly 'mountain' road took place and Martin's Singer rocketed up to win his class outright *and* on handicap. The little car was even quicker that day than the 2-litre DFP (Doriot, Flandrin et Parant) driven by one of two brothers who imported the marque from France. (W.O. Bentley, who frequently competed with DFPs, would soon be building cars bearing his own name, as would Martin. Bentley's last *magnum opus*, the 2.6-litre Lagonda engine, was to be the key to the success of the cars which are the subject of this book.)

It was Robert Bamford who adapted a small Isotta Fraschini chassis to take one of Pelham Lee's 1.4-litre side-valve Coventry Simplex engines — the ancestors of the Coventry Climax — although Lionel Martin was the one who influenced the concept of the new marque. The project had hardly got off the ground when war came. Bamford and Martin made their next prototype immediately afterwards, but it was not until March 1921 that *The Autocar* gave the new 'light, sporting car, the

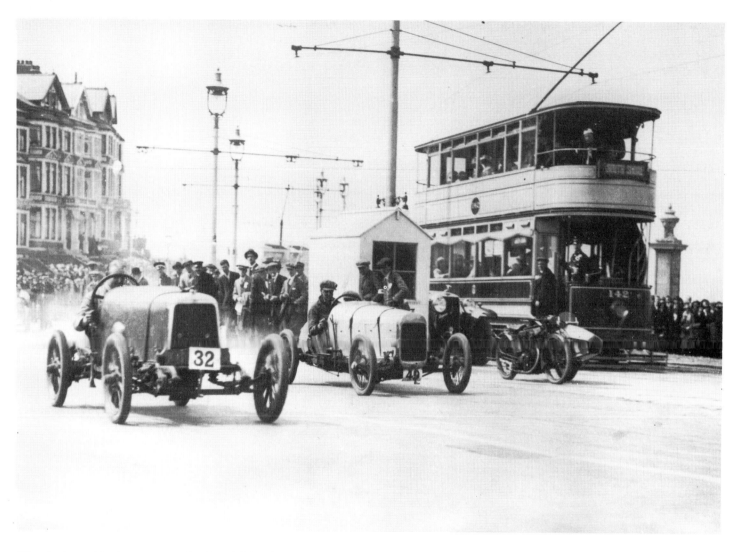

All early Aston Martins were sporting 'specials', only about 60 being made between 1914 and 1925, including 'Bunny' (car 32), seen here out-accelerating Beardsall's Hodgson in a 1924 sprint on Queen's Promenade, Blackpool, when driven by Eddie Hall. He had acquired it after it had completed three years as a works team car.

Aston-Martin, the result of experience gained by Mr Lionel Martin applied in conjunction with data obtained from the use of a great number of well-known cars' its first publicity in the form of three editorial pages. (It is worth noting that, for many years, the use or otherwise of a hyphen between 'Aston' and 'Martin' remained totally inconsistent, whether reference was being made to the firm or to its products. Before the hyphen was specifically omitted, the company sometimes allowed both forms to appear within the same advertisement.)

By 1920 Bamford had left the company. However, with money and technical advice from well-known and wealthy racing drivers — notably the American-Polish Count Louis Zborowski — the Aston Martin name gained fame through a series of out-and-out competition models created by Martin. Although these were more complex overhead-camshaft designs, including one Peugeot-based 16-valver, the prototype side-valve racer called 'Bunny' (a name which had been applied prewar to several racing Singers) was the most successful in the early days; Stead's second place in the 1922 Brooklands 200-mile race at over 86mph was the result that made a particular impression.

Probably as a result of Zborowski's death (in a Mercedes in the 1924 Italian GP), the true financial situation became apparent. After all, when a big firm like Morris was boycotting racing on the basis of the cost and time involved in doing it properly, how could Aston Martin — building an average of one or two production cars a month — hope to make money *and* compete in the 'big time'?

The Aston Martin was shown for the first time at the 1925 motor show at a chassis price of £625; if the lesson had been learned it was too late. Bamford and Martin Ltd (as the firm was still registered) of Abingdon Road, off London's Kensington High Street, was declared insolvent almost immediately afterwards, in November 1925. This would not be the last occasion on which Aston Martin went missing from the UK car price lists, presumed dead. The Martin era was over; the Bertelli era was about to start.

What remained of the company was in the hands of the Hon John Benson, later Lord Charnwood — no mean engineer himself — whose family money, with Zborowski's, had been the main means of keeping Aston Martin afloat. Meanwhile, Augustus Bertelli (who had known Martin well from their shared interest in racing) and William Renwick (formerly an Armstrong-Siddeley trainee) were setting-up in business, Renwick having been left enough money to rent premises in Birmingham.

Augustus Cesare Bertelli, born in Italy in 1890, but brought up in Wales from the age of four, was thoroughly British. His engineering experience was considerable, including design work (and some motor racing) which helped the short lived Enfield Allday marque live a little longer than it might have done otherwise.

It was in an Enfield-Allday chassis that Bertelli's new overhead-camshaft 1½-litre 'four' was tried first of all, the original idea having been that Renwick and Bertelli would supply engines to the motor industry, although the possibility of making complete cars was not ruled out.

What marked the Bertelli era, from 1926, was the excellence of the engineering, but the financial instability never went away. Bertelli and Renwick moved south from Birmingham, and Benson joined them at a new location in Victoria Road, Feltham, Middlesex. Bertelli moved quickly, and the new Aston Martin range was launched at the 1927 show at Olympia, with a £465 price tag for the chassis. His brother Enrico moved, too, from Wales to adjacent premises at Feltham. There, for the next decade or so, he turned out some of the most exquisite low-slung bodywork to be seen on a British sporting car. Prices at that show were £550 for the tourer and £675 for the saloon.

While the brothers got on with the job in hand, Renwick and Benson appear to have fallen out; both of them left, Benson being the one to go first. Several people put money into the company to help keep it running, but there were still occasions when the wages were not paid.

Frazer Nash cars were produced nearby, the firm being run by H.J. Aldington, who, with his two brothers, had taken over from the ailing and unbusinesslike founder in 1929, having already been involved with the marque for some years. Then Aston Martin hit another crisis and Bertelli sold out to Aldington in February 1931. Aldington took over control of sales and of the official entries for the Double-Twelve Brooklands race. The Frazer Nashes did not perform well on that occasion, but Aldington — whose money helped to build the works cars (LM5/6/7) — took home the trophy when the Aston Martins came 1-2 in their class. However, Aston Martin sales did not improve

Racing has been in Aston Martin's blood from the beginning. This nicely preserved short-chassis 1933 1½-litre was driven by Petit and Esson-Scott in the Mille Miglia over 50 years ago.

quickly enough, and Aldington decided to either wind-up or sell-up. After a holding operation by a dealer, Sir Arthur Sutherland took over at Feltham in 1932. A son, Gordon Sutherland, was appointed to share management of the company with Bertelli, who developed the marque into a highly reputable one. A dry-sump '1½' was followed by both wet and dry-sump 2-litre units, still to Bertelli's overhead-camshaft design, from 1936. Bertelli left that year, without warning, being unwilling and unable to work with Sutherland, who wanted to make a more docile road car. Augustus Bertelli stayed with engineering, but not with motor cars, and lived to a ripe old age.

His successor in charge of Aston Martin engineering was Claude Hill, who had worked for him and Renwick as a junior draughtsman in the Birmingham days, had later moved south with them and had become Bertelli's right-hand man. Hill had left once, when there was no money in the kitty, but after less than a year with Morris Engines he had responded to a plea from Bertelli to return.

Sutherland was the ideas man; Hill put the ideas into practice. The Aston Martins of the late 'Thirties never had the aesthetic attraction of (say) the 1935-36 sports-saloon, but they were technically interesting. The streamlined Speed Model was not a pretty car, nor were the ones-off 'Donald Duck' and 'Atom' four-door saloons — the latter being so-called (according to the late Claude Hill) because Gordon Sutherland said it was a small package with a big performance. This car was later purchased by Nigel Mann and went to France. These four-door saloons were given wide press coverage in the early war years when

A few of the Claude Hill 2-litre 'fours' were given this rather ugly bodywork in the late 'Thirties. These two Type Cs, photographed at an AMOC Silverstone celebration, are former works cars — LMF 387 (G40/718/U) and KMP 533 (F9/721/U).

Possibly the most active of all Aston Martins, and one of the last to be built before Bertelli left, is John Freeman's Speed Model EML 129 (J6/707/U). Tony Rolt was racing it in 1938 and St John Horsfall brought it home fourth in the 1949 Spa 24-hour race. The Stapletons drove it in the 1951 and 1952 Mille Miglia races, and then the Freemans ran it regularly in club events from 1955. It is seen here competing at Silverstone.

Sutherland's eye to publicity for the future was not outweighed by the aircraft industry contract work which occupied Hill for the duration. Afterwards, Hill developed the 'Atom' theme of combining a tubular body frame with the main chassis, which featured independent front suspension. In a move away from the traditional overhead-camshaft design, Hill drew a new shorter-stroke overhead-valve unit; it was still a 2-litre four-cylinder.

Money was short and progress on Hill's long-wheelbase 2-litre sports (the car we now tend to call the DB1) was slow. Sutherland

put Aston Martin on the market in 1946. David Brown, head of the famous gear-making group, read about it in *The Times*, went to Feltham for a look, and for £20,000 bought the prototype, a few rusty old machine tools and the services of Claude Hill . . . just for fun.

Soon afterwards, a Yorkshire Lagonda distributor suggested to Brown that he might make a second purchase. At first he was not interested. A former amateur motor sportsman himself, David Brown had admired Aston Martin's successes at Le Mans in the 'Thirties, and the same went for Lagonda, but its image was quite different; it was not as appealing to this sporting tycoon, and anyway, it looked very much as if William Lyons of Jaguar, or even one of the bigger Coventry groups, was about to pounce. Lagonda went into liquidation in 1947 and the factory had already been sold when Brown agreed to take a look. With all the other serious bidders out of the way because of the high suggested price and the poor economic situation, David Brown had a clear run, but he actually raised his bid from £50,000 to £52,500 as a gesture of goodwill. He leased some hangars on Hanworth airfield, near his newly acquired Aston Martin premises, and moved his Lagonda assets, such as they were, into them.

Before moving into the David Brown era of the Aston Martin and Lagonda firms, it is only fair to mention the main reason for Lagonda's collapse, for Alan Good had been in charge during its greatest (V12) period.

In 1945, as one of his last acts for Lagonda, Dick Watney insisted on announcing the new LB6 as the Lagonda-Bentley. Rolls-Royce were up in arms because they had bought the right to use 'Bentley' themselves. 'W.O.' had a diplomatic chat with Lord Hives, of Rolls-Royce, but this was nullified by Alan Good putting his oar in. The resultant lawsuit cost Lagonda £10,000, which was a lot of money in the 'Forties. It is logical to conclude that this was why Alan Good got out of the motor car business. Good thrived on his image of success. Some wag once said that if he was not seen smoking one of his enormous specially made Dunhill cigars, or at least a Players Perfectos, as he walked through a factory, he believed his employees would think he was going broke. It is also said that although Alan Good's death in 1953 was through overwork, burning the candle at both ends had also played its part. Nevertheless, if it hadn't been for Alan Good and Gordon Sutherland, there would not have been a Lagonda, or an Aston Martin, for David Brown to acquire.

CHAPTER 2

New life for Lagonda

Maintaining the luxury image

Whatever production plans had been laid for it, the postwar Lagonda, though complete in its general design, was far from ready when David Brown took over. In fact, four years would pass from the original LB6 (Lagonda-Bentley) announcement of autumn 1945 to the first definitive road tests of what was called, simply, the Lagonda 2½-litre.

No postwar production of the magnificent prewar models — 'sixes' or '12s' — had occurred; the company's financial position had seen to that. The David Brown purchase included the name, the drawings, the parts and the prototypes — but not the premises.

The design by W.O. Bentley and his helpers was both classical and modern. The major announcements were three-quarters of a page in *The Autocar* on September 14, 1945, followed by two full pages in *The Motor* of September 19. The latter was headed: *A New 2.6-litre Lagonda — Advance Announcement of an Entirely New W.O. Bentley-designed Car for the Post-War Market.*

Most of the description related to the engine, already defined as a 2,580cc six-cylinder, but the car itself was clearly well advanced, too, though the illustration showed only the power unit on test, watched by Bentley (puffing at his pipe), Donald Bastow, Charles Sewell (designer) and Stanley Ivermee (experimental department). Deliveries of the new cars would not begin until (according to *The Autocar*) 'towards the end of 1946'. That forecast was to prove over-optimistic.

W.O. Bentley had studied the motor industry's products not merely as an engineer, but also as a market researcher. His idea was *not* to place Lagonda in direct opposition to Rolls-Royce (or Bentley!) as he had with the V12, but to make a slightly smaller, lighter and less expensive car for an equally fastidious and possibly more sporting clientele.

As mentioned previously, it was the LB6 engine design which went ahead. This was unique, when it was first described fully in the press in the winter of 1946-47, in having double overhead camshafts. Jaguar's XK twin-cam would not be seen until 1948; the only other British make to use the configuration was the stillborn Invicta Black Prince, designed by William Watson, who had done so much of the LB6 design work for W.O. Bentley. Elsewhere, only Italy's Alfa Romeo and the French Salmson would offer double-camshaft engines to the public in the immediate postwar years.

The prototype LB6 was at the test and refinement stage when war ended. Rated at 22.6hp for taxation purposes, the 2,580.5cc (78×90mm) six-cylinder engine was one of the few automotive units anywhere to provide over 100bhp. It also met the Bentley requirement of smooth, silent running which had been such a feature of the V12 prewar. Features included detachable wet liners and near-hemispherical combustion chambers. The angle between the inclined valves was 62 degrees, and use of a direct camshaft/tappet/valve layout made adjustment of clearances a rare chore. The crankshaft had four bearings carried in separate split annular housings, the whole assembly being slid into the crankcase from the rear. (The block-cum-crankcase was made extra-rigid to compensate for any potential weakness of the wet-liner design.)

A none-too-satisfactory feature of the early engines was a blade-type chain tensioner. For production (at the David Brown works in Huddersfield) a patented tensioner — hydraulically

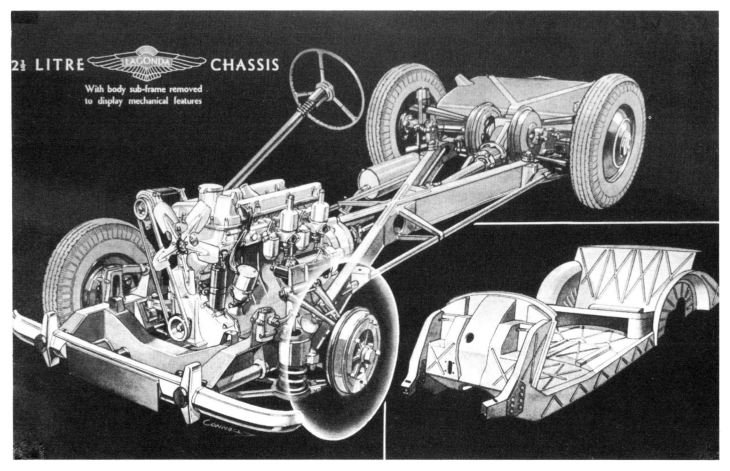

2½ LITRE ⬥ LAGONDA ⬥ CHASSIS

With body sub-frame removed
to display mechanical features

Reproduction from a Lagonda sales catalogue showing the chassis layout and the design of the body subframe.

operated from the main pressure feed — was incorporated. Alloy pistons were well-domed, low octane ratings dictating low compression ratios in those days.

Patents were sought for quite a number of aspects of the new car's design, although not all were followed up. Modifications could cloud issues. Rigidity was the theme of the cruciform chassis frame design, its main members being I-section beams $6\frac{1}{2}$ inches deep.

All-independent suspension was specified throughout the project's gestation period, and as late as 1953 *The Motor* described the Lagonda's rear seat ride (if not the car's behaviour) as being 'unapproached by any other comparable British car'.

Interior of the prototype 2½-litre Lagonda showing the control for the Cotal gearbox protruding from the centre of the dashboard. Although it appeared in the catalogue, this form of transmission was dropped before the car went into series production.

Unfortunately for Lagonda, that state of affairs was not to last for very much longer, but in its day the specification was both attractive and unique. Independent front suspension was by double wishbones and coil springs — a sturdy and straightforward enough arrangement — but the rear end was more complicated and underwent many development changes. The suspension here was by a form of swing-axle system, with a pair of torsion bars mounted along the angled cruciform frame members. The stub axles were carried by large ball-jointed tubular wishbones but, to reduce unsprung weight, the brake drums were placed inboard, adjacent to the hypoid differential casing. The drive shafts were, naturally, universally jointed. On the original design they were intended to trail, but they were placed at right-angles to the car's centreline for production. The car tended to oversteer, but good rack-and-pinion steering helped to alleviate the problem.

The prototypes, the original leaflets, and the first descriptions all featured the Cotal electro-magnetically controlled four-speed constant-mesh gearbox, the small lever first being placed on the dashboard, but then transferred to the steering column.

Production prototype of the 2½-litre Lagonda, identifiable by large quarter-lights in the front doors and by side-lamps built into the top of the wings. At the rear, the number-plate was recessed into the bootlid.

23

The definitive 1950 Lagonda saloon featuring smaller front quarter-lights and a plain bootlid, the number-plate being mounted between the bumper overriders.

The dashboard of a 1950 Lagonda. For the Mark II version, which was introduced in 1952, the instruments were moved in front of the driver, leaving the heater control panel in the centre and a large single cubbyhole on the passenger's side.

Normally, the Cotal box had a reverse facility built in for all ratios; for the Lagonda this was omitted and replaced by a separate epicyclic reverse gear as part of the final drive. A Newton automatic centrifugal clutch was fitted to one prototype and specified in the first catalogue. At an early stage petrol injection was considered, but it was dropped in favour of twin SU carburettors before David Brown's arrival.

The body shape had been settled by then, too. Frank Feeley

(who had joined his father at Lagonda in 1926) had established himself as a stylist of individuality when he drew the 1937 LG45 Rapide for his then boss, Dick Watney. His equally attractively curving body for the V12 saloon of 1938 formed the basis for that of the LB6 prototype. This definitive postwar Lagonda curved even more. In January 1947 it was described as 'graceful' and 'modern'. (Indeed, it never lost its grace, but 'Baroque' became a more accurate description as postwar full-width bodywork established itself as the norm.) A Ford adjunct, Briggs, was to have made the bodies, but they changed their minds and became one of the main reasons, along with the 'Bentley name' court case, for Lagonda going into receivership. This was when 'W.O.' retired to Weybridge and, helped by Donald Bastow and others, carried out design work on a consultancy basis, notably for Armstrong-Siddeley.

Sir David Brown has claimed that he instigated a change in engine size from 2.3 to 2.6 litres, but in fact all the main features, including the capacity, remained the same under the new regime. Brown also went on record as having found five LB6 prototypes, whereas the figure of three seems more likely. Certainly, a serious test programme was initiated in the early part of 1948 and it led to one major change — the fitting of an alternative manual gearbox and orthodox clutch. (Autumn 1948 saw the Cotal box still listed, but it never went into production.)

David Brown had already acquired Aston Martin and, before that, his family business had undertaken occasional work for the motor industry. His grandfather had started his pattern-making factory in 1860, but by the time the 17-year-old David began his apprenticeship, in 1921, the speciality was the manufacture of gears for industry. Although father was not keen on the idea, David Brown introduced the company to tractors in 1936. Soon he led the Huddersfield-based industrial giant, and felt he could

Even more attractive than the saloon, the 2½-litre Lagonda drophead coupe recalled the grace of the immediate prewar bodywork. Unfortunately, the stoneguard on the rear wing has already suffered a small dent.

The Mark II 2½-litre Lagonda saloon. Note the flush-fitting instead of the earlier recessed rear windows, the rear number-plate, which has been repositioned again on the bootlid, and the revised rear door shut line.

The larger rear door was a welcomed feature of the Mark II saloon. The revised instrument layout is also in evidence here. The chauffeur is demonstrating the operation of the pump handle for the Jackall lifting equipment. Note the useful boot capacity and the low loading height.

begin to indulge in the occasional diversion.

Putting Lagonda back on the map was not going to be easy, but Brown (he would become *Sir* David in 1968) could utilize his well-established Yorkshire facilities to make the engine, which he had also earmarked for Aston Martin use, and, of course, the manufacture of a synchromesh gearbox 'in-house' was equally logical.

Lagonda records show that three early production cars were

The earlier column shift has given way to a central gear-change on this late 3-litre chassis, which has been prepared for display purposes.

The cruciform chassis for the 3-litre Lagonda introduced in the mid-'Fifties was virtually unchanged from W.O. Bentley's design for the 2½-litre car. Note the inboard-mounted rear brakes.

The introduction of the 3-litre chassis brought a widening in the range of body styles, this two-door saloon supplementing the restyled four-door saloon and drophead coupe models. (Photograph courtesy of *Motor*.)

allocated to Gurney Nutting, including one as a chassis and another with the Cotal gearbox, and the implication is that this famous coachbuilder was to tool-up on behalf of the new Lagonda company. The frames and the bodies, however, were built at Hanworth Park, Feltham, largely by former Staines men under Frank Feeley, who still admires Gurney Nutting styling, but is sure it had nothing to do with postwar Lagonda.

Thanks to David Brown's ability to get the necessary steel allocation, production got under way at Hanworth Park. There were talks about drophead coupes being made by Tickford (formerly Salmons) of Newport Pagnell, but they were not to come into the picture yet.

Although Aston Martin had been purchased first, it is interesting to note in a late 1947 advertisement that the Lagonda illustration was clearly based on a completed body, whereas the 'Aston Martin 2-litre sports' was shown by a hurried schoolboy impression of remarkable shapelessness. (Company names were not mentioned; at the foot of the page were the words 'Products of the David Brown Tractors Group'.)

From the outset a Lagonda drophead coupe had been planned,

and it was this type which was first road-tested by *The Motor* for its issue of September 14, 1949. Reading between the lines, the poor top gear acceleration came as a disappointment, it being pointed out that 'when the design was laid down, all cars were subject to a heavy tax based on engine size'; and the 'inevitably high wind resistance' was mentioned in relation to the 'admirable achievement' of a mean maximum speed of just over 90mph. It was found that the clutch was heavy, that third and fourth gears were best regarded as 'top' and 'overdrive', respectively, and the reader was recommended to consider the Cotal gearbox — an 'option' which, in fact, would never be available to the customer! The woolly steering-column gear-change probably led to that remark.

Apart from anything else, the Lagonda's weight of nearly 1½ tons unladen helped to limit the performance. Only a few weeks earlier, the same basic engine had provided Aston Martin with a very satisfying third place in the Belgian 24-hour race, so the unit's capabilities were in little doubt among the pundits. What impressed the testers so much was the great smoothness, even at higher engine speeds.

The stiffness of the frame, the lack of squeaks and rattles, and above all the ride came in for the highest praise. 'No car which has yet been through our hands, quoted *The Motor*, 'has equalled the postwar Lagonda in combining supreme comfort, particularly in the rear seats, with stability and good handling qualities.' Indeed, the only real faults found were a lack of lateral support, cubby holes and fresh air ventilation.

The Autocar's findings during their saloon test (November 11, 1949) were similar. Their particular talking point (and there was rarely much room for talking points in the three-page road tests of those days) were the steering and the effect of rear wheel movement upon it. One can only surmise that, having frightened

A pronounced rear overhang offered the owner of a 3-litre Lagonda exceptional boot capacity, while flush filler caps in each rear wing were a reminder that the car's thirst for fuel was also considerable.

themselves by their discovery of keen oversteer, they drove a little more sedately and found out what a superb car the Lagonda was to ride in. This particular car, UMC 382, was the first UK-registered saloon, and the original factory sales records note (without comment) that it was 'later damaged at Ferrybridge'. Readers with memories of that particular stretch of the old A1 road in Yorkshire, or even familiar with it in its awkward re-

alignment today, can probably imagine just where an emergency situation might catch-out the fast, heavy Lagonda with its suspension working overtime.

From 1949 to 1952, Lagonda production managed to drag itself up to an average of three to four cars a week, usually including one drophead coupe. Relatively few chassis were supplied unbodied although Graber of Switzerland was a notable

Polished walnut dashboard and door trims were in keeping with the luxury image of the 3-litre Lagonda, this example of which retains the steering column mounted gear-change. (Photograph courtesy of *Motor*.)

recipient in November 1951.

Chassis numbering began at LAG 48/1, indicating the year of manufacture, but there were very few with the '48' or '49' prefix. The sequence runs: LAG 48/1 to 48/12, LAG 49/13 to 49/74, LAG 50/75 to 50/76, LAG 49/77, and then LAG 50/78 to 543, indicating that the year-change idea had been dropped. LAG 48/1 had body number 18001, synchromesh gearbox number DBR/48/1 and engine number LB6/48/7.

The first two saloons were recorded out to the David Brown Tractors Group, and the first drophead coupe — a metallic green publicity car, SMX 10 — was passed to Mrs Brown in July 1950. The first three exports were to Australia, one customer being B. Sellar Stillwell — surely racing driver 'Bib' Stillwell's father? One of the three cars was returned to the UK. (When I was a boy, the swooping lines of the new Lagonda impressed me greatly when a local dignitary by the name of Wotherspoon bought one. My home town, Inverness, was a place where any new or different type of car caught one's attention in those days. That car, it turns out, was the failed Australian export, HSC 700.) Exports to the USA were unsuccessful, too, although Max Hoffman, who monopolized Jaguar, Volkswagen and many other imports, did show a chassis at several exhibitions.

The price of the Lagonda was higher than W.O. Bentley had intended, but the long gestation period made that pretty academic and it fluctuated in the early days.

Autumn 1952 saw the arrival of the Mark II version of the 2½-litre Lagonda, which met most of the press criticisms of its predecessor. There were still no door pockets, but there were practical cubby holes elsewhere, *and* a proper heating and demisting system. Better seating adjustment and armrests were featured and, in the rear, 4in was added to the seat width. The rear door was wider, too, opening from the centre of the wheelarch rather than ahead of it. Another recognition feature was the fitting of more distinctive Lucas headlamps. A relative novelty was the incorporation of a Smiths Jackall jacking system with sufficient travel to deal with the droop of all-independent suspension.

The UK tax-included price was £2,996. Normally more expensive, the drophead coupe was now listed at £40 less, but no Mark II coupes were to be made, though this may not have been a conscious decision at the time.

Improved it was, but demand for the Lagonda was flagging, and the price didn't help. British customers looking for a distinctive and sporting four-seater in that autumn of 1952 had some interesting choices. For less than £2,000 it was possible to buy a Light Six AC, a 3-litre Alvis, or one of the new Armstrong-Siddeley Sapphires. Compared with the Lagonda, the Jensen Intercepter was slightly cheaper, the Bristol 401 slightly more, but both were quicker — and you could buy a new Bentley or Rolls-Royce for little more than £3,500. Moreover, since its announcement 'for export only', two years earlier, the 100mph $3\frac{1}{2}$-litre twin-cam XK-engined Mk VII Jaguar was now being sold in the UK for an inclusive £1,775, with automatic transmission (a basic Borg-Warner two-speed, it's true) only just around the corner. In fact, only a few Mark II Lagondas were made, and production petered out in the summer of 1953.

Comparing the information available at the Newport Pagnell factory and at Aston Services Dorset, the following Lagonda $2\frac{1}{2}$-litre production figures seem to be reasonably accurate:

Between October 1948 and July 1952

Saloons (Hanworth-built)	302
Drophead coupes	118
Saloons believed assembled by Tickford	57
Chassis	7
sub-total	484

Between September 1952 and July 1953

Saloons, Mark II	10
Drophead coupes	0
Chassis	16
sub-total	26
Grand total:	510

The figure of 510 is apparently at odds with a final chassis number of LAG 50/543, but there is a note which indicates that 23 cars were made with 3-litre engines and possibly new-style bodies (LAG 1 to LAG 23) during this period. A final drophead coupe figure of 125 is made possible by the existence of a body number 28125; so, the inference is that at least 500 2.6-litre Lagondas were made, but not many more.

This uncertainty of the numbering during 1953 may, perhaps, be put down to David Brown's acquisition of the Salmons Tickford coachbuilding business in Newport Pagnell, where the new Lagonda's body would be made. At this period much of the chassis work was undertaken in 'David Brown territory' rather than in Middlesex, there being more space and better manufacturing facilities in the Group's factories around Yorkshire — in this instance at Farsley, between Leeds and Bradford.

The differences between North and South manifested themselves at this time, and perhaps it was inevitable that Newport Pagnell — neither North nor South — should become the eventual headquarters!

Frank Feeley recalls that it was industrial action that brought the Middlesex side of the operation to an end from a body manufacturing point of view. He reckons it was such action that finished Weymann (later taken over by Metro-Cammell) and that Aston Martin Lagonda had acquired some of the same trouble as a result. Attempts to resolve wage disputes by people going to Yorkshire for money just wouldn't work. (The early Aston Martin DB2-4 bodies would be made by Mulliners of Birmingham in the end.)

June 1952 had seen the W.O. Bentley engine being raced in enlarged form for the first time when the Aston Martin DB3 ran (briefly) at Monaco — but it was in a Lagonda that it made its debut as a series-production power unit.

Compensation for the petering-out of the Baroque-style Lagondas came with the announcement at the 1953 Paris show of completely restyled two-door saloon and drophead coupe models. The engine had a bigger bore and a nominal power output of 140bhp at 5,000rpm. The dimensions were now 83×90mm and the swept volume was up from 2,580 to 2,922cc — so, whether one reads of '2.9' or '3-litre' engines in DB stories, one is reading about the same thing. Compression ratio was up

Arguably the most handsome 3-litre Lagonda of them all, the drophead coupe, which retained a rare elegance whether the hood was raised or folded. Tickford coachwork at its best.

The author at the wheel of a 3-litre drophead coupe which carries its 30 years remarkably well.

Two ages of transport and each suggesting a certain refinement. Note the sharp angles of the door windows of the coupe.

The walnut picnic trays mounted on the front seats are another reminder of a time when life carried on at a rather more leisurely pace.

from 6.5 to over 8:1.

The Lagonda 3-litre (or 'Tickford', as it was usually dubbed) would almost certainly have pleased 'W.O.', though he was no longer with the company. It kept his wet liners and his four-bearing crankshaft, but to keep an even water jacket William Watson offset the bores, which, in turn, meant offset connecting rods. The twin SU carburettors were enlarged from $1\frac{1}{2}$ to $1\frac{3}{4}$in

diameter, with manual choke control.

While the chassis was essentially of the same design and dimensions as before, the body was now 8in longer and $1\frac{1}{2}$in wider, and this led to a weight increase of more than 2cwt. Nevertheless, the true maximum speed was now well over 100mph. (There had been a couple of slab-sided prototypes, the 'Red Monster' and the 'Blue Monster', also styled by Frank

A look beneath the bonnet of the same 3-litre drophead coupe. Note the twin batteries flanking the heater installation.

Feeley, but the 3-litre was the first full-width Lagonda to reach production.)

Once again, the drophead coupe version was instantly appealing, visually, and in due course it would become the more familiar model, HRH Prince Philip being the often-photographed owner-driver of two in succession.

The reason for the slight reservations about the saloon's looks arises from the high waistline. This effect is often an attractive feature, but when a car's occupants are also seen to be sitting high the effect *can* be incongruous. The overall height of the new Lagonda was kept down to 62in (about 2in less than its predecessor) yet the floorpan, sitting on top of the cruciform chassis, could go no lower without creating awkwardly shaped wells — probably in the wrong places for feet.

After the 3-litre there was a considerable pause before the Lagonda name reappeared with a 4-litre Rapide, the last of the six-cylinder models and produced in very small quantities on a modified Aston Martin DB4 chassis, as is explained more fully in Chapter 7.

Although the same length as the Mk VII Jaguar, the 3-litre Lagonda was a good 6in shorter in the wheelbase than the Coventry car. Indeed, the Lagonda was so close-coupled that, when a four-door model was brought in (to overlap with and eventually replace both two-door types), the front seat-backs could still be tilted forward to help rear passengers in and out with decorum.

The quiet good looks, the luxury and the quality were without question, but the specification — so good on paper — was looking a little less certain in this particular (and very small) marketplace. There was never any kind of automatic transmission option. The manual gear-change was improved for a 1956 Series II version by its removal from the outmoded steering column location to the floor, but heavy clutch operation continued to attract mild rebukes from the car's few press road-testers. Steering and braking were hard work, too; the Lagonda still oversteered and, with little effort, the Lockheed servo-assisted hydraulic brakes (inboard at the rear, remember) could be made to fade. Disc brakes were under development at Aston Martin Lagonda, but the 3-litre Lagonda would disappear before they could be fitted. Moreover, the engine — with its whining camshaft drive — was noisier than it should have been in this kind of car.

In the autumn of 1956, the Series II Lagonda 3-litre four-door saloon was listed at £3,901 including Purchase Tax, the drophead coupe being priced at £4,501. Then, on the eve of the motor show, David Brown announced huge price cuts to £2,994 and £3,376, respectively. The prices were still high, however. Jaguar brought out their new Mk VIII at nearly £100 (model for model) above the price of the Mk VIIM — and with Jaguar you had the options of manual, manual-with-overdrive and automatic transmission, the latter being the most expensive at £1,998. The Lagonda had dipped below the £3,586 of a Bristol 405 saloon, but it was more expensive than Jensen's Interceptor (£2,701) or the Graber-bodied Alvis (£2,776). The Lagonda may no longer have been up in the Silver Clouds (the regular Rolls-Royce was now £5,244), but that drastic price cut was a distinct sign of cutting of losses.

David Brown had still not achieved his ambition to win Le Mans, either with the Aston Martin or with an abortive V12-powered 'Lagonda'. However, it was not the end of the road; the David Brown Group had the capacity to absorb more losses for the time being, but something had to be done. Aston Martin road cars needed updating, too, and what new-model money there was, was already being ploughed into the DB4 project.

The DB4 and other subsequent Aston Martins would lead to the creation of several cars bearing the Lagonda name, which David Brown had acquired so reluctantly, but now seemed bent on perpetuating. The 3-litre, which died quietly in the winter of 1957-58, was the last truly individual Lagonda with any kind of brand loyalty attached to it.

Looking at the records, I have interpreted the following output for the 3-litre Lagonda during its lifespan from 1953 to 1957:

Series I drophead coupes (1953-56)	50
Series I chassis (to Tickford)	1
Series I 2-door saloons (1953-55)	70
Series I 4-door saloons (1954-56)	68
Series II drophead coupes (1956-57)	5
Series II 4-door saloons (1956-57)	76
3-litre Lagondas of all types	270

I have seen a figure of 420 published, but can find no basis for it.

The subsequent 4-litre Rapide did not live up to the great name it revived. In total, 55 were made (including eight for export) between 1961 and 1964. They were the last six-cylinder Lagondas to be built; their persistence on the production line (and therefore their drain on resources) was probably related to John Wyer's failure to establish an operable merger with the Alvis company. That last Lagonda Rapide was, in fact, to be one of the main reasons for the resignation of John Wyer — a key man in the saga of the DB Aston Martins, to which this story now reverts.

CHAPTER 3

Brown's Beauty — the DB2

Competition success lays the foundation

While this book is essentially about the David Brown six-cylinder cars, it would be wrong to begin the Aston Martin part of the story without mentioning the pushrod 'fours' and their competition successes, which were brief, but memorable.

All prewar Aston Martins had had four-cylinder engines. In the Bertelli period they had been classic overhead-camshaft units of $1\frac{1}{2}$ and 2 litres. Then there was the Sutherland period, with its awkward styling and its inventive engineering by Bertelli disciple Claude Hill. The most famous of those prewar attempts to modernize the sports car was the Atom, which looked like the Bentley Corniche saloon in miniature and (as W.O. Bentley's 1945 Lagonda would) featured a Cotal gearbox.

David Brown did not rush into anything straight after buying Aston Martin and its works in the early part of 1947. Later that year, when he bought Lagonda without its Staines factory, and moved that company into hangars at Hanworth Park, Feltham, Middlesex, close to the Aston Martin premises in Victoria Road, Feltham, it became clear that he saw Aston Martin and Lagonda as the respective sporting and luxury cars of a range to be produced by the David Brown Tractors Group ('Tractors' was deleted from the wording after the first few advertisements). The Lagonda design was the first to be given the go-ahead, because it was so far advanced; the only major change there was was the replacement of the Cotal gearbox by a 'DB' unit.

The Aston Martin situation was much more tentative. At first it seemed that David Brown would give Claude Hill a free hand. Brown wanted to see Aston Martins racing; he had observed the success of St John Horsfall and others in the 'Thirties, and again in 1946, when Horsfall won the first postwar 2-litre sports car race in the *Bois de la Cambre* parkland in the heart of Brussels. Horsfall was a great driver and Brown brought him in, on a retainer, as chief tester.

The combination of Claude Hill's engineering and 'Jock' Horsfall's test and race proving of the chassis was the most significant single factor in the making of the postwar Aston Martin's reputation for chassis rigidity and superb handling. Horsfall recommended a lightened version with a skimpy body for the 1948 Belgian 24-hour race, which he promptly won, Leslie Johnson sharing the honours, which included the BRDC's trophy for the year's best performance by British drivers abroad. 1948 also saw the production Aston Martin 2-litre (as it was described officially) being launched almost simultaneously with the Jaguar XK 100 and XK 120. Like those cars, it had a flamboyant open two-seater body with divided windscreen and a sweeping wing line.

Unlike Jaguar — who majored on the six-cylinder XK 120 and would soon forget about *their* 2-litre 'four' — Aston Martin did not offer a 'six' at the 1948 Earls Court show, although Claude Hill had in fact been working on one. Brown's immediate reaction was to point out that *he* had one already — just across the road, in fact! Moreover, the Lagonda-Bentley engine, with its twin overhead camshafts, had a more sporting specification on paper. Claude Hill's pride was hurt by this, and soon after his pushrod six-cylinder had been turned down he left the company. (Subsequently, Freddy Dixon contacted him, and this led to Hill becoming Chief Engineer at Ferguson Research — later to become F.F. Developments and run by sometime Aston Martin and Jaguar racer Tony Rolt. Hill stayed there until his retirement

138

in 1971.) Only 15 production versions of the Hill-designed, Feeley-styled 2-litre Aston Martin were built. This was the car which is known, retrospectively, as the DB1; there was no such name for it when it was current.

Before Hill left, however, his chassis design had been modified and clothed in a gorgeous modern coupe body — the work of Frank Feeley, the Lagonda body designer with whom David Brown got on so well. This compact car had a wheelbase 9in shorter than that of the DB1 at the recommendation of Horsfall who, having left Aston Martin, was to be killed racing an ERA at Silverstone that August.

Three coupes were built initially, and they made their public debut at Le Mans in June 1949, for David Brown had decided that his sports car company must contest France's first postwar 24-hour race. Two of the cars had Hill's 2-litre engine, the other being fitted with Bentley's twin-cam unit and thus becoming the first-ever six-cylinder Aston Martin. It was to be driven by Charles Brackenbury and Leslie Johnson, but it covered only six laps before a design fault in the water pump caused it to run dry long before the minimum replenishment distance had been covered.

A fortnight later, however, the same car (Chassis No LML/49/3, registered UMC 66) came third overall in the Belgian 24-hour race. Indeed, with a little luck, Brackenbury and Johnson might have won because Luigi Chinetti's little 166 Ferrari, leading the Spa event, spun on oil spilled by Louveau's expiring second-placed Delage and hit a building. The incident came near enough to the end of the race to allow both cars to struggle on and

Two views of the flamboyant 2-litre Aston Martin which was the work of Claude Hill and Frank Feeley and, retrospectively, has often been referred to as the 'DB1'. This example, AMC/49/6, became the 1949 Earls Court show car.

Having won the Index of Performance at Le Mans in 1950, the DB2 became a centre of attraction in export markets as well as at home. This car, and the 2½-litre Lagonda right behind it, were leaving the Staines factory to begin their journey to the United States. (Photograph courtesy of *Motor*.)

finish without losing their positions; the very same cars had finished first and second at Le Mans, too. (Had there been any kind of European Championship for sports cars in 1949, Louveau's 3-litre Delage might well have won it; but the writing was already on the wall for that once-great French marque.) In contrast, the Aston Martin was about to come alive again, thanks to David Brown and his DB2 — or '2½-litre saloon' as he called it in his post-Spa advertising.

Had *Gran Turismo* then been a part of the language of motoring, there is no doubt that the new car would have been

hailed as its epitome when it first appeared. In addition to the three race cars, a fourth coupe — the second '2½' — was prepared with a more civilized interior. Early in 1950, this car (LML/49/4, registered UMC 272) was taken on a 1,000-mile continental trip by *The Motor's* Technical Editor, Laurence Pomeroy, who was quite as impressed by this 'Le Mans-type' Aston Martin as by the gastronomic experience *en route*. This car was then bought from its regular user, David Brown, by Lance Macklin, who had it fitted with Weber carburettors in time for the Coppa Inter Europa on March 26, this two-hour race on the Monza circuit

The production-type DB2 body is being carried on VMG 606. This car (LML/50/5) was originally equipped with a 2-litre engine, but acquired an LB6 late in 1950. The prominently framed front and side grilles were also a feature of the 'VMF' works cars initially, although these were subsequently altered. The DB2 UMC 66, alongside, illustrates the differences to be found on cars numbered 49/1 to 49/4. On the extreme left of the picture is HX 4323, Inman Hunter's famous 1931 works Le Mans car, LM7.

being open to sports and touring cars. Grand Prix driver Consalvo Sanesi finished first for Alfa Romeo, followed by Stagnoli and Cornacchia in Ferraris, then in fourth place overall came Macklin in his new Weber-equipped Aston Martin, which he then drove south for the Targa Florio exactly a week later.

In 1950, the Targa Florio and Giro di Sicilia road races were combined and instead of several laps of the Madonie mountain circuit it took the form of a single lap of Sicily — one giant special stage (in today's terms) of about 670 miles. Early in the race,

Macklin misread the road ahead and launched out into space. Fortunately, a drainage ditch prevented the wrecked car actually landing at the bottom of a railway cutting. Incidentally, that race also saw the demise of Jaguar's XK 120 on *its* first continental race sortie; Clemente Biondetti ran second to Alberto Ascari (Ferrari) before the Jaguar retired due to a broken connecting rod. Jaguar and Aston Martin were to become great but fairly friendly rivals as Britain's leading representatives in international sports car racing over the next six years. With no

45

modern Aston Martins present, it was former Aston Martin driver Leslie Johnson who gave Britain and Jaguar fifth place overall in the Mille Miglia three weeks later.

In 1948 and 1949, John Eason Gibson had been retained to manage David Brown's racing activities. Now Laurence Pomeroy passed the word to John Wyer (who had recently sold his business, Monaco Motors of Watford) that David Brown was looking for a Team Manager. Wyer arrived at Feltham in time to organize the team's arrangements for the 1950 Le Mans race, this coinciding with the resolution of a production specification for the car and the settling of its name — DB2.

The first true production car (LML/50/5, indicating the year change, registered VMG 606) was kept by the company, then sold secondhand to former Allard rally driver Geoffrey Godsal, who promptly crashed it on the 1952 Alpine Trial.

The Lagonda engine — manufactured at the Meltham, Huddersfield, works of David Brown — was virtually unaltered for the DB2 in production form. Regular fuel was still of low octane value, and would remain so until the introduction of 'premium' in 1953. Power output for the 6.5:1 compression ratio unit was quoted as 105 or 107bhp at 5,000rpm, with torque of either 125lb/ft at 3,100rpm, or 130lb/ft at 3,000rpm.

During 1950, the obsolete word 'Vantage' was brought back to identify a high-performance engine option. This unit had a compression ratio of 8.16:1, and again two contemporary sets of figures can be quoted: 123bhp at 5,000rpm (144lb/ft torque at 2,400rpm) and 125bhp at 5,000rpm (149lb/ft torque at 3,000 rpm.) The first road test car (adding somewhat to the confusion) was a 1950 team car, for which *The Motor* quoted 116bhp at 5,000rpm and a 7.5:1 compression ratio.

The David Brown four-speed gearbox was offered with the choice of steering column or floor-mounted lever, the latter being fitted to the works competition cars and those of the more discerning customers. Suspension was still, essentially, the development by Claude Hill of his own design for Sutherland's Atom a decade earlier. The trailing-link and coil-spring independent front suspension featured a transverse anti-roll bar enclosed by a hollow front structural member and connecting the two lower suspension links. Coil springs were used at the rear, too, where the live axle was located by parallel arms and a Panhard rod. The concensus of critical opinion was that the

handling and roadholding on good surfaces were superb up to very high limits, but that the suspension became — not unnaturally — less supple where the going was rough. This did not prevent the DB2 from obtaining some outstanding and generally unsung rally results at international level. The cam-and-roller steering enhanced the feeling of tautness and security, as did the 12in Girling drum brakes, which nevertheless juddered under heavy use over long distances.

Early road tests by *The Motor* and *The Autocar* were carried out on works cars which had seen competition use, whereas *Motor Sport* was loaned the official demonstration car (LML/50/10, registered VMF 37) which was the prototype DB2 drophead coupe; and it leaked — providing 'WB' with his only serious adverse criticism. He found the brakes to be fierce and noisy, but powerful, too, and his overall impression probably summed-up everyone else's — that here was a veritable magic carpet with which to shrink the roads of Europe, or what the enthusiast would call, simply, a real motor car. 'It is no exaggeration to state that it stands out as one of the world's really great cars', wrote William Boddy, without adding any qualifying remarks. Without a doubt, the name of Aston Martin was regaining the cachet it had acquired in its most stylish days of the later Bertelli era — and it would progress a lot further, too.

The DB2 in competition
David Brown's determination was insufficient, on its own, to make his cars successful in racing. The man who, more than any other, enabled the sporting industrialist to realize his dreams was John Wyer.

John Leonard Wyer was born in 1909 in Kidderminster and apprenticed to the Sunbeam Motor Company in nearby Wolverhampton, his father being an agent for the famous marque. He joined in 1927, just missing the company's great racing days, and stayed on briefly after his apprenticeship as a junior draughtsman. Sunbeam had never recovered properly from the worst of the slump; Wyer saw it going downhill and left in the mid-'Thirties, shortly before the Rootes brothers strode in. He gained experience in India and France as an engineer for Solex Carburettors, who promoted him to a London management job. He left at the end of the war, and moved closer to motor racing as a partner in Monaco Motors. In 1948, he ran

Three views of UMC 272 (LML/49/4) in course of restoration for its present owner, Peter Lee, by Aubrey Finsburgh, of Classic Autos. Originally the works development car, this was possibly the first Aston Martin to receive an LB6 engine. Built in 1949, it was crashed in its second race, the 1950 Targa Florio.

An underbonnet view of UMC 272 with the characteristic bulkhead water tank prominently displayed. The tow rope around the water pipe was not a standard fitting!

the pit at Spa-Francorchamps for his colleagues Ian Connell and Dudley Folland, who were driving the latter's 12-year-old 2-litre Aston Martin, and it was then that he first came to know David Brown. Two years later he joined him.

The DB2 was already well-known in sporting circles when Wyer arrived at Feltham. If motor racing was to be the company's policy, then there would have to be a proper development programme and a purpose-built car. That was clear. Meantime, however, Wyer was charged with the task of getting results with the DB2, for the first of the new breed of Aston Martin sports-racers was still over a year away. The DB2 was race-bred, but the 'Bentley' 2.6-litre engine just did not have the capacity to give hope for an outright victory, and David Brown wanted more than mere class victories. It was to be a long road, and Aston Martin would take nearly the whole decade to

achieve its ultimate goal. Along the way, however, the Aston Martin racing team helped the marque's reputation *and* it often obtained good results.

Le Mans in 1950 was John Wyer's first race as team chief, and it produced for him an unexpected victory in the Index of Performance category; but it had started badly, for Jack Fairman managed to roll one of the three brand new beauties (LML/50/9, VMF 65) into a French orchard during the drive south. Fairman was freed to look after his pregnant wife in hospital — she had injured her back in the inexplicable accident — and reserve driver John Gordon was brought in to take his place alongside Eric Thompson. They had to make do with the spare car (LML 49/3), only to retire early.

The other two cars — LML/50/7 (VMF 63) for Reg Parnell and Charles Brackenbury and LML/50/8 (VMF 64) for George

The production DB2 had no conventional boot, but at least there was a little room in the spare wheel hatch. The subtle rear body curves were to be lost when the body was converted into a hatchback later on.

Abecassis and Lance Macklin — set a standard for consistency and reliability. Although French Talbots dominated the race from start to finish, once an early Ferrari challenge had faded, British cars led the rest of the field.

A Jaguar XK 120 looked like taking second or third place until its clutch broke in the 22nd hour. Then it became a fight between Allard and Healey with their big American engines. However, the Aston Martins were never far behind and, in fact, Abecassis and Macklin were in the top six throughout the second half of the great marathon, despite a lengthy stop to deal with a sticking throttle linkage. Besides sharing the Index of Performance prize (with a French Monopole) the leading DB2 broke the 3-litre distance record, which had been held by a Delahaye since 1939.

The results of Le Mans 1950 were quite satisfying, particularly when it could be noted that the surviving Jaguars had to be content with 12th and 15th positions. The leader-board at the end of the race read:

1st Talbot-Lago	4.5 litres,	3,465Kms
2nd Talbot-Lago	4.5 litres,	3,440Kms
3rd Allard-Cadillac	5.4 litres,	3,389Kms
4th Healey-Nash	3.8 litres,	3,385Kms
5th Aston Martin	2.6 litres,	3,370Kms
6th Aston Martin	2.6 litres,	3,294Kms

One under-3-litre car which could compete with the early DB2

An immaculately presented DB2 chassis on display at Earls Court in October 1951. Note that this example has the floor-mounted gear-change. (Photograph courtesy of *Motor*.)

on level terms was the Healey Silverstone, upon which the Healey-Nash Le Mans car had been based. It was an open two-seater, powered by the 2,443cc Riley four-cylinder engine, and it had shown a good turn of speed when driven by Tony Rolt at the first one-hour Silverstone production car race in 1949. When the second of these events was held in August 1950 a tremendous battle developed between Duncan Hamilton in his Healey Silverstone and the Aston Martins of Raymond Sommer (deputizing for the injured Lance Macklin in LML/50/8), Reg Parnell (LML/50/7) and Eric Thompson (LML/50/9) for victory in the 2-3-litre class, Hamilton narrowly taking the honours after Sommer had spun on oil from Peter Whitehead's

sick Jaguar.

September 1950 was a busy month for Aston Martin. Prior to Le Mans, Macklin and Brackenbury had put in some practice with the first of the DB2 team cars on the high-speed Linas-Montlhéry circuit. The performance had been satisfactory, and so, on September 5, 1950, at 6pm, an assault on a series of long-distance International Class D records began at the famous Paris track, Brackenbury, Macklin and Thompson being nominated to drive. The weather was foul and getting worse, but about 107 miles were completed in the first hour, and after 500 miles the average was 103.79mph. Then visibility became so bad that Wyer had to bring the attempt to a premature end, but not before

The DB2 in its attractive drophead coupe form. The revised grille with horizontal bars, introduced in 1951, considerably improved the frontal appearance of the car. (Photograph courtesy of *Motor*.)

Two views of Dr Nicholas Storr's drop-head coupe LML/50/203, which was originally shipped to Belgium in the Spring of 1953. An excellent example of a most attractive car.

This close-up of the cockpit of Dr Storr's coupe reveals that at one time it was fitted with a steering column-mounted gear lever. Conversion to a central shift is common practice amongst DB2 owners.

the DB2 had proved itself capable of lapping the banked track at 117mph relatively easily.

By September 16, the team was in Ulster for the first postwar TT race, which was being held on the exciting Dundrod road circuit in the hills above Belfast. As at Silverstone, the XK 120 Jaguars were untouchable, but the Aston Martins were almost as dominant in their own class, beating the Healeys handsomely, helped to some extent by the comfort of an enclosed cockpit, for the race was held in torrential rain. The DB2s seemed to handle better than any other cars and their high-calibre driving trio entertained the crowd, if not their Team Manager, by their dexterity — Macklin went down the Cochranstown escape road, and Abecassis regularly put his car nearly broadside. After three hours, the TT gave the Aston Martins this result:

4th on distance and handicap, 1st in class, LML/50/7 (Parnell)

5th on distance and handicap, 2nd in class, LML/50/9 (Abecassis)

7th on distance and handicap, 3rd in class, LML/50/8 (Macklin)

A week later, the three works DB2s appeared, rather surprisingly, at the Shelsley Walsh hill-climb, where Abecassis, Parnell and Brackenbury came fourth, fifth and sixth, respectively, in the 1½-3-litre production car class, giving best to the drivers of three of the very agile Le Mans Replica Frazer Nashes, whose power-to-weight ratio and compactness were seen to best advantage. As a road-going GT car, however, the DB2 was a much more attractive proposition (even though LML/50/9, competing in that November's MCC Rally, got nowhere, despite being driven by Lance Macklin and Stirling Moss).

1950 had been a frustrating season. Truly, there was no car

53

The trio of works DB2s — VMF 63, 64, and 65 — setting off after Stirling Moss' Jaguar XK 120 in a downpour which was to last the duration of the first postwar Tourist Trophy race at Dundrod, in 1950. Moss' victory that day was a high point in his rapidly developing career. Note that the Aston Martins still have their early vertical-bar grilles.

comparable to the Aston Martin, so it could not show its true worth. Excellent performances went relatively unnoticed because they did not represent 'first across the line'. The success at Le Mans had been worth a lot, however, and David Brown had demonstrated his recognition of John Wyer's capabilities by inviting him to stay on indefinitely as Racing Manager, with added responsibilities for engineering development. Clearly this was not just an enticement, but an indication that Aston Martin needed specialist engineering talent urgently.

There were still niggling undercurrents of the kind that afflict all mergers. Both Aston Martin and Lagonda had David Brown to thank for their survival and for the employment he provided, yet some of those steeped in the history of each marque found it difficult to adapt. This is a familiar situation in an industry where the stamp of the individual contributes to the character of the whole. Gone were the Walter Bentleys, the Claude Hills and their engineering disciples. On the production side, James Stirling and his assistant James Watt were getting things under way, but in whose hands lay the future of Aston Martin and Lagonda design?

Two engineers of particular significance joined David Brown Tractors' car division towards the end of 1950. One was Robert Eberan-Eberhorst, whom we shall meet in the next chapter, and the other was a Londoner called Harold Beach. His background was built on an apprenticeship with the ancient and revered coachbuilding firm of Barker. As Barkers fell behind the times, Beach moved on, first to spend three years as a draughtsman with the Wimbledon subsidiary of William Beardmore, Beardmore-Multiwheeler, who had manufacturing rights for the French Chenard-Walcker tractor unit. However, diesel engines and drawbar trailers didn't hold Beach's interest very strongly, and so he joined one of his old Barker colleagues in a small coachbuilding shop, where his chief claim to fame was the design of the body for Eddie Hall's famous Rolls-Bentley which got so near to winning the Ards TT on three occasions in the 'Thirties.

Then it was back to multi-wheelers with the Hungarian, Nikolaus Straussler, and his military vehicles and equipment made in Middlesex in conjunction with several established manufacturers (including Alvis, whose postwar six-wheelers resulted from the Straussler connection). Straussler was an experimenter whose peacetime plans did not meet with the success of his materials for war. In 1950, in response to a *Daily Telegraph* advertisement, Harold Beach's itchy feet took him to Feltham. His long service to Aston Martin and Lagonda would be one of the essential ingredients for continuity in the years to come.

Meanwhile, John Wyer had to face another full season of racing with the DB2, for Eberhorst needed to get his feet under the table and put on his thinking cap, and that would take time.

The most famous works DB2, VMF 64 (LML/50/8) was raced and rallied extensively before being purchased by the Hon Gerald Lascelles. This picture was used widely to publicize its great third place at Le Mans in 1951, by which time it had acquired a production-style grille.

Tom and 'Bill' Wisdom used VMF 64 in the 1951 Alpine Trial and not only won their class with it, but also secured a coveted *Coupe des Alpes* for a penalty-free run. (Photograph courtesy of *Autocar*.)

David Brown gave Wyer approval for building two new DB2s, 350lb lighter than their predecessors.

Aston Martin was not yet ready to enter the Mille Miglia officially, but Fleet Street journalist (and excellent driver) Tom Wisdom persuaded David Brown to lend him *his* car for it in 1951. This was LML/50/8 (VMF 64); the other two 1950 team cars had already been pressed into service for road tests by magazines including *The Motor* (VMF 63) and both *The Autocar* and *Autosport* (VMF 65). VMF 64 acquitted itself well, Wisdom (accompanied by Anthony Hume) coming 11th (and first in class), though well behind winner Villoresi's Ferrari and indeed several smaller-engined GT cars; for example, Bracco was second in a Lancia Aurelia.

Looking even more attractive, with redesigned radiator grilles, the two new racing DB2s were entered for the *Daily Express*

Silverstone one-hour race to be held in early May. They were faster than their predecessors, but only marginally — and the same could be said for Jaguar and Healey. (Once again the Frazer Nashes were racing against each another in a separate class.) The new cars were LML/50/50 (XMC 76) and LML/50/55 (XMC 77) and they were driven by Parnell and Abecassis, respectively. Their lightness came, in part, from the use of alloy cylinder heads, but these gave trouble and were not to be used again. Abecassis had a huge spin on the pits straight, due to gearbox seizure, but Parnell won the 2-3-litre class easily and was seventh overall behind five Jaguars and the Healey-Nash of Tony Rolt.

It was clear to Wyer by this time that the new competition car would not be ready for Le Mans, so he borrowed VMF 64 back from David Brown. He couldn't get it as light as the two new DB2s, but some 200lb was taken out of it. The main mechanical difference between the 1950 and the 1951 Le Mans cars was the fitting of three double-choke Weber carburettors in place of the regular twin H6 SUs. Between Silverstone and Le Mans the power output figure went up from 128 to 138bhp, and this, plus reliability and a good manager-driver relationship, was to give Aston Martin its best result for many a year.

Historically, 1951 is regarded as Jaguar's year at Le Mans. Coventry sprung something of a surprise with the new C-type, and it won the race easily. What the records also show is that four Jaguars started, but only two finished; five Aston Martins started and they *all* finished.

After four hours, the works Jaguars were 1-2-3 and the best Aston Martin was 10th, but after 12 hours only one works C-type remained (leading) and the same Aston Martin — the previous year's car, VMF 64 — lay fifth and ready to challenge all but the Jaguar. John Wyer set an average lap speed for the whole race, as he had done in 1950, only quicker, and the Aston Martin which came third overall in 1951 (at a higher average speed than the 1950 winner) was within three seconds-per-hour of its target at the end of the race, which produced this excellent result for Britain and for Aston Martin:

1st, Jaguar	3.5 litres, 3,612Kms
2nd, Talbot Lago	4.5 litres, 3,486Kms
3rd, *Aston Martin*	2.6 litres, 3,477Kms
4th, Talbot-Lago	4.5 litres, 3,463Kms
5th, *Aston Martin*	2.6 litres, 3,449Kms
6th, Healey-Nash	3.8 litres, 3,449Kms
7th, *Aston Martin*	2.6 litres, 3,402Kms
10th, *Aston Martin*	2.6 litres, 3,196Kms
11th, Jaguar	3.5 litres, 3,187Kms
13th, *Aston Martin*	2.6 litres, 3,152Kms

Only 30 cars were classified as finishers from 60 starters. Driver pairings for the works Aston Martins (which came 1-2-3 in their class) were: 3rd, Macklin/Thompson (LML/50/8); 5th, Abecassis/Shawe-Taylor (LML/50/55); 7th, Parnell/Hampshire (LML/50/50).

The new team members, Brian Shawe-Taylor and David Hampshire, were two of the outstanding ERA drivers of those days. The DB2 privateers at Le Mans were Peter Clark with Mortimer Morris-Goodall (10th) and Nigel Mann with Jack Scott (13th).

Never before or since have Aston Martins shown such complete reliability as in that 24-hour race, and after it, the TT was something of an anti-climax. Macklin retired the new DB3 and Brian Shawe-Taylor (LML/50/50) was beaten in the 3-litre class by Ulster newspaper magnate Robert Baird (2.6 Ferrari), following the retirement of Abecassis (LML/50/55) with clutch failure. Jaguars filled the top places, Shawe-Taylor was seventh on the road and Thompson eighth in the older car. Both lightweight DB2s were running on SUs again for this race.

Perhaps to give mainlanders a late-season look at the cars, or maybe because Aston Martin drivers enjoyed social/sporting venues, Abecassis and Parnell attended the September Shelsley Walsh meeting with DB2s, taking 44.15 and 44.95 seconds, respectively, for the climb.

Mille Miglia class winner Tommy Wisdom had been loaned VMF 64 again for the Alpine Trial in July, and he had put up another sterling performance to win a coveted Coupe des Alpes — the standard prize for a penalty-free road run. Just beforehand, Gordon Wilkins had tested the already-famous car for *The Autocar*, discovering the effects of its special preparation, mainly in the form of roughness in traffic and shattering performance away from it. The mechanical noise inside the enclosed bare-metal cockpit with its sliding plastic windows was, he found, pretty shattering, too — although he was able to note a distinct lack of wind noise and draughts. After Wilkins' test, the car had been put back to road trim, including twin SU carburettors, for Tommy Wisdom and his wife 'Bill' to take on their Alpine sortie.

That had been VMF 64's last major event of 1951. Then it became clear that the DB3 would not be ready for the start of the 1952 season, which began for the lightweight DB2s with a first and a third for Eric Thompson (XMC 76) and Dennis Poore (XMC 77) in an Easter Goodwood handicap sprint race. VMF 64 — LML/50/8, the most famous DB2 of all time, was made ready for battle, too — for a third season! This work was in the hands of the service department, whereas two 'lightweights' were prepared by John Wyer's men in the competition shop. Wyer admitted later that he had not been at all pleased at first to see David Brown's support for Wisdom, whose excellent results had

The 1956 RAC Rally winner, Lyndon Sims, takes NGO 651 (LML/50/X2) through one of the Blackpool tests. His navigator on that event was Tony Ambrose, who later was to become a leading co-driver in the BMC rally team. (Photograph courtesy of *Autosport.*)

subsequently made him change his mind, to the extent that Wisdom was actually treated as a member of the team when Mille Miglia time came round again. What was more, he scored the best result for Aston Martin!

Accompanied by Feltham mechanic Fred Lown, Wisdom had an uneventful 1952 Mille Miglia and completed the course a good half-hour sooner than he had the previous time; he finished 12th overall and won his class again.

As in the TT, George Abecassis (LML/50/55, XMC 77)

retired — the clutch broken. Reg Parnell (LML/50/50, XMC 76) went off the road early on, but he nursed his car to the finish to come 13th and second in class, just beaten by the steady Wisdom. John Wyer left Italy sharing David Brown's admiration for the chain-smoking scribe.

The 1952 Mille Miglia had been a battle between Ferrari and Mercedes-Benz, the latter giving the 300 SL its impressive debut with a second and a fourth place overall. On the way home, the two lightweight DB2s paused in Bern, Switzerland, to take part in a sports car race in which the new German cars dominated proceedings. The fast, wooded and somewhat treacherous Bern circuit was well-known to motorcycle champion Geoff Duke, and although this was his first continental car race he led Parnell throughout. The final order was Mercedes-Benz 1-2-3, driven by Karl Kling, Hermann Lang and Fritz Riess in that order, then came Duke in XMC 77 and Parnell in XMC 76.

After Bern, the lightweight DB2s reverted to development work at the factory, although they reappeared for the 1953 Mille Miglia, XMC 76 being used for team practice, while XMC 77 was lent to Tommy Wisdom in the hope of a hat-trick of class wins. As part of their preparation they were fitted with 3-litre engines, but both cars gave trouble, and Wisdom had to retire when the rear axle gave up; he continued to drive the works 'lightweights' in 1953 and 1954, but without success.

By this time, however, the DB2 had acquired a high reputation which was fully justified. It was in full (though very low-volume) production, and was confirmed as the car that had put Aston Martin on its feet.

Some private owners competed in speed events, and the DB2's superb manners often flattered the capabilities of its driver. Up to this time, Wisdom's 1951 Alpine performance had been the highlight of a rather sparse international rally career, and not until 1956, when it was well and truly obsolete, would the DB2 gain its biggest outright win — the RAC Rally, in which Lyndon Sims and Tony Ambrose made history for the marque, and pushed the famous team of Ian and Pat Appleyard (Jaguar XK 140 coupe) into second place.

For most of its later life, however, the DB2 became more bland, to provide Aston Martin with its bread and butter. Its successor, the DB2-4 (as it was called), was a fine car without the charisma — to this writer at least — of Frank Feeley's inspired original, the fabulous Aston Martin DB2, one of the outstanding designs of its day.

The personal registration number JB 16 indicates that this is Jean Bloxam driving her DB2 up Prescott hill in 1957. Later, the car (LML/50/199) was bought back by its original owner, Major Woods, from Jersey; the DB2 is that kind of car.

These two pictures, taken by the author in the Silverstone paddock during 1983, indicate clearly that owners of DB2s not only look after them with meticulous care, but also believe that their rightful place is on the race track, even if only in club events. For many years, members of the Aston Martin Owners Club have been at the forefront of this branch of the sport.

CHAPTER 4

The DB3

Aston Martin's first sports-racer

The Aston Martin DB3 was a good competition car, but it was not a great one. It achieved only one big win, and was raced as a works team car for just one year, between the *Daily Express* Silverstone meetings of May 1952 and 1953. Yet the DB3S, which succeeded it — and which was not, technically, so very different — undoubtedly qualifies as one of the great British sports-racers.

Even the identity of the DB3 has been mistaken many times. The final version of the DB2 was the DB2-4 Mk III. This mouthful was abbreviated, officially, to DB Mk III and often, unofficially, to DBIII, or even DB3. Thus the real DB3 is relatively unknown today, whereas the DB3S is something of a legend.

Another DB3 paradox is the fact that its creator, engineering professor Robert Eberan von Eberhorst, *was* a truly great designer in his own right. He was also a great theorist, whereas David Brown's technicians were more used to the idea of meeting each deadline — often 'tomorrow' or even 'yesterday' — in the best way they could.

Robert Eberan was Austrian, but a refugee from East Germany after the Russians came. He was tall, elegant and thoroughly gentlemanly. His first claim to international fame was his work with the V12 Auto-Union cars of 1938. Even in his old age, he would attend motor shows with one of the few rebuilt GP Auto Unions, patiently answering questions about those amazing Saxon machines. If ever he acted the *prima donna*, as has been suggested, then it was not evident to those less close to him than his Aston Martin colleagues of the early 'Fifties.

Indirectly — and as with Wyer — it was *The Motor* Technical Editor Laurence Pomeroy who brought Eberan to David Brown's door in 1950. Pomeroy had first befriended Eberan before the war, and in 1948 he went to Turin to see him when his first postwar project — the building of the Porsche-designed flat-12 Cisitalia GP car — was foundering. Meanwhile, racing driver Leslie Johnson had acquired the ERA name, and from May 1949 he was to engage the services of Eberan as his Racing Development Engineer. Used to having at least some tools for his trade, the professor was somewhat taken aback when he found at ERA's Dunstable base not a proper factory, but what he was to describe as 'a backyard garage, with no tools, no test-beds and no money', as a result of which he was 'loaned' to Jowett to design the chassis for the car which was to become the Jupiter. Another bit of sub-contract work arranged between Pomeroy and Brown led to Eberan acting as consultant to Aston Martin Lagonda one day each week. There he established an excellent working relationship with the technical chief, James Stirling, who helped Eberan out of a distinctly awkward contract he had with Johnson. By the end of 1950, the professor was ensconced in the Feltham works as Chief Engineer.

It seems certain that the Austrian engineer and his British counterparts were at cross-purposes from the start. Never mind the budget, how could a new sports car be designed over one winter and made ready for next summer's Le Mans? Maybe Jaguar, in creating their XK 120C, were trying to do the same thing, but they had a potentially more integrated racing management team and an engine ready for the job with little change. Although both men had set their hearts on winning Le Mans, there was one particular aspect of their approach which

First time out for the DB3. Lance Macklin, driving DB3/1, keeps an eye on the pursuing DB2 saloons as he leads the 3-litre group away at the start of the 1951 TT at Dundrod.

made David Brown and Jaguar's William Lyons as different as chalk and cheese. Lyons was *not* making cars, *nor* racing them, for fun.

Eberan and Wyer maintained a healthy respect for one another without ever agreeing on basic policy. The first DB3 was not ready in time for Le Mans, so instead, a single car made its debut on September 15, 1951 in the TT at Dundrod, following the briefest of tests at the MIRA test track and having been hand-painted only after its arrival in Belfast. Driven by Lance Macklin, it was fourth fastest in practice behind the three works Jaguars, but the Aston Martin was scarcely race-ready and although Macklin ran second to Moss on handicap for a while, the DB3

retired after 27 laps due to bearing failure, although at the time there was vague talk of 'a broken exhaust'. So Stirling Moss and Jaguar won the TT for the second year running — but Aston Martin's Dundrod day would come.

The DB1 and DB2 had had elements of Claude Hill's Atom in their structures, but the DB3 was all-new and all-tubular — more reminiscent of Auto-Union and Jowett Jupiter, in fact! The latter had a triangulated arrangement of tubes over the back axle and featured transverse torsion bars at the front.

The front suspension of the DB3 was independent, of course, with trailing arms and an anti-roll bar. The rear-end assembly was on the de Dion principle, located by a Panhard rod with parallel links to counteract torque.

Alfin brake drums were fitted, these having proved fairly satisfactory on the two lightweight competition DB2s (and VMF 64 in later life), whereas Jaguar had considered them but had then decided to go all-out with Dunlop on disc brake development. On the DB3, the rear drums were mounted inboard, much to John Wyer's alarm. Laurence Pomeroy backed Robert Eberan's decision in print, though his tones were more guarded than usual: 'Scoops in the undershield direct air currents both on to the rim and on to the face of each brake drum and expert opinion has testified that despite apparent enclosure of brakes in this position it is actually easier to cool them than when they are placed on the hub, but partly shrouded by the rim of the wheel.'

The engine was the well-proven 2.6-litre of Bentley origin, with triple Weber 36 DCFS carburettors standard and greater oil capacity provided in its ribbed alloy sump. Another visible difference was the new timing chain cover; this permitted a low

Peter Collins with co-driver Pat Griffith took DB3/5 to victory at Goodwood in the 1952 nine-hour race. This was the best-ever win for the 2.6-litre DB3.

Reg Parnell and Louis Klementaski, sitting in DB3/3, get a last word from Clerk of the Course Renzo Castagneto at the start of the 1953 Mille Miglia, in which they were destined to finish fifth.

bonnet line which contributed to a frontal area of 13sq ft compared with the DB2's 18sq ft.

Although not very distinguished-looking, the open envelope body had a nicely curving tail; the radiator air intake managed to retain the elements of the shape which had always been a characteristic of the marque, and 1952 began with high hopes for the DB3.

Two new drivers joined the team at this stage — Peter Collins and Geoffrey Duke. Duke had never raced cars before, and his debut was with the sole DB3 to run at the Goodwood Easter races of 1952. It was something of a tradition to see new features being tried out at this meeting, which marked the opening of the UK season, and Stirling Moss was racing a C-type Jaguar with disc brakes for the first time.

The Duke and Moss 'duel' gained a lot of prior publicity, but the handicapping of their six-lap sprint was poor. Two Jaguar XK 120s fought for the lead throughout and provided the main interest, but they never looked like being caught, even though Duke drove the DB3 well to take third place. However, the star of that meeting was Mike Hawthorn, making instant news by his driving of the new Cooper-Bristol.

The same prototype DB3 appeared at Ibsley, Hampshire, a week later in the hands of Dennis Poore, who gave it its first win. The runner-up in this seven-lap race was Roy Salvadori (Frazer Nash) who, like Poore, would become a works Aston Martin driver before long.

It was at the *Daily Express* meeting on May 10 at Silverstone that a full team of four DB3 Aston Martins first appeared, but in spite of some trouble with the experimental disc brakes, Moss in the works Jaguar kept the new cars at bay. Of the Aston Martin team, only Duke in the prototype (DB3/1) broke formation by spinning on someone else's oil and then spinning again due to damaged steering. The other DB3s took the team prize by finishing second, third and fourth driven by the 'old firm' of

The mystery coupe number 76 in the middle of the pack in a club race at Goodwood is, in fact, DB3/5, the 1952 nine-hour race-winner, which had been rebodied for its new owner Nigel Mann. More recently, and running without the hardtop, this car has become a familiar sight in historic races in the USA, driven by Tony Goodchild.

Parnell (DB3/3), Abecassis (DB3/4) and Macklin (DB3/5), respectively. Silverstone had been a short race — barely 50 miles — and serious warning of the bad times to come was not given until May 29, when Geoff Duke was given the tidied-up DB3/1 for the British Empire Trophy race — 200 miles on the slow, bumpy, Douglas street circuit. Duke led the field and made the best lap time of the day, but then he stopped on the circuit with ignition trouble; in due course he came into the pits, then tried a few more laps, but the crankshaft broke at half-distance.

An interesting new race on the 1952 calendar was at Monte Carlo, where the Monaco Grand Prix was staged as a sports car event over 100 laps, representing very nearly 200 miles of street fighting. Monaco strained relations between Eberan and Wyer to the limit, and it was as well that David Brown was a great one for putting failures behind him and getting on with the next thing. Everyone realized that the 2.6-litre engine had its limitations — not least William Watson, who had done much of W.O. Bentley's

original spadework on it, and who had come back to work as Senior Design Engineer under Eberan von Eberhorst. Watson went to see Wyer as early as 1951, anticipating the problem with a scheme to enlarge his engine to 2.9 litres. His Austrian boss would not agree to it, and much time was lost, as a result of which it was not until Monaco, on June 2, 1952, that the 3-litre Aston Martins raced.

Practice was cool, but the race was hot. Reg Parnell and Peter Collins (having his first drive for Feltham) were soon pit-callers, in need of radiator water, as Moss (Jaguar) led from Manzon (Gordini) and a host of Ferraris.

At quarter-distance, Manzon took Moss for the lead, just as Parnell (DB3/3) was sliding into the barriers with a seized engine. Several drivers failed to get adequate warning, including Manzon and Moss, who cannoned into the *mêlée*. (There are some famous photographs of drivers hopping to safety.) After 73 laps, Macklin (DB3/5) had to give up, and the upshot was a

Ferrari walkover, with the reliable Tommy Wisdom coming sixth in his new C-type Jaguar, followed by Peter Collins (DB3/4) a distant seventh. Virtually as it crossed the finishing line, the Collins car broke a connecting rod, just as Parnell's and Macklin's had done. Because the cars had been driven out, replacement engines were flown out for two of them, while the Parnell car was sent to Paris by train for repair.

Despite reversion to 2.6-litre engines for Le Mans on June 14-15, the DB3 team was not out of the wood yet. Parnell and Thompson drove DB3/1, fitted with a fastback coupe top, and they were among the first to drop out when the hypoid rear axle seized. The same thing happened to Collins and Macklin (DB3/5) when they were running fourth early on Sunday afternoon.

The third works DB3 was a very strange-looking rebuild of DB3/3. It had been whisked away from its Paris workshop to replace the designated car (DB3/4) which newcomer and Empire Trophy winner Pat Griffith had put off the road

expensively in practice. Due to the necessary haste, DB3/3 arrived at the circuit with a short tail section — quite different from the car which had been through scrutineering with the same number. No-one said anything and the car started in the race, only to be brought in after four laps by Griffith's co-driver, Dennis Poore, with the beginning of chronic gearbox trouble, although the car's actual withdrawal on Saturday evening was attributed to the water pump.

1952 marked the return of Mercedes-Benz to Le Mans, and it was unfortunate for Britain that its two top teams — Aston Martin and Jaguar — should be eliminated in the very year when a stirring battle should have taken place. With the Italian teams in trouble, only the streamlined French Talbot-Lago of Pierre Levegh presented a threat, and it held a four-lap lead for most of the second half of the marathon. Levegh was trying to win single-handed, however, and history will always blame tiredness and missed gearchanges for his car's retirement with about an hour to go. All of a sudden, memories of the 'Thirties and the Mercedes Method of Motor Racing came flooding back as the silver coupes cruised to a surprised and surprising victory.

Two Aston Martins, still with their 2.6-litre engines, were entered for the Jersey road races on July 10 and the Boreham international meeting on August 2. Abecassis (DB3/4) and Parnell (DB3/5) were third and fourth in the final at St Helier, having been third and second in their respective heats. Up to this time, the DB3 had always run with its unreliable David Brown Type S527 five-speed gearbox, as originally specified. However, for Jersey and thereafter the DB3 (and its successor, the DB3S) reverted to the old but effective four-speed, the David Brown Type S430.

At Boreham, in August, Parnell (DB3/5) came third in the 10-mile sports car race to win the 2-3-litre class from Roy Salvadori and Tom Cole in 2.7-litre Ferraris, but Abecassis (DB3/4) retired with a blocked fuel filter. As at St Helier, the overall winner was a C-type Jaguar, this model now beginning to appear regularly in private hands to supplement the Coventry works effort.

Unexpectedly, the persistence of the team and the patience of David Brown were about to pay off, with a DB3 giving Aston Martin its first outright win in an international long-distance motor race since the marque had graduated from four cylinders to six. The first BARC Goodwood nine-hour race was run from 3pm to midnight on August 16, 1952, and promised to be a fascinating event, even if the 'international' element was thin by comparison with Le Mans. It provided plenty of excitement — *and* considerable pain for three members of the DB pit team, John Wyer and two of his leading hands, Fred Lown and Jack Sopp, all of whom had to be whisked off to hospital with serious burns from a fire in the pit lane which could have killed someone.

Eric Thompson had been circulating in the short-tailed DB3/3 with an over-hot rear axle — a function of the temperatures generated by the inboard rear brakes. Goodwood was hard on brakes; indeed, it was an exacting circuit in many ways. In the damp early stages, Parnell had passed all the Jaguars for a while, going like the wind with a new 2.9-litre engine to help him. Thompson was third when he came in after 93 laps to hand back to Parnell. A rear axle seal had begun to weep, and hot oil now lay steaming in the undertray. It was not a time for careless

Angela Brown being chased by Peter Sargent's Jaguar XK 120 during a North Staffs MC meeting at Silverstone in 1955. Sir David Brown's daughter, who was to marry Aston Martin team driver George Abecassis, had bought the car, DB3/7, from Tom Meyer, for whom the special body, suitable for long-distance racing, had been made in 1953.

refuelling, but that is precisely what happened, and within a moment the whole car had become a ball of flame. It was lucky that there were only the three hospital cases.

The nine-hour race ran its course, with two works Jaguars seemingly in full control — only to run into trouble with stub-axle and rear A-bracket breakages late in the race. A second DB3 (2.6 litres, DB3/4) had already retired with a broken clutch but, suddenly, the surviving car (2.6 litres, DB3/5) was in with a chance. Its main opponents now were two 2.7-litre Ferraris, one of which could have been leading if Roy Salvadori had not lost time off course. Cunning Reg Parnell, who had taken over the pit from John Wyer, also managed to get the Ferrari pulled in because of inoperative tail-lights. All this gave the youthful Peter Collins an opportunity to nurse his car to the finish despite running on only five cylinders by then. With co-driver Pat Griffith, Peter Collins had won the first really long race to be held in Britain since the war. It may have been a lucky win, but it was not undeserved.

There was no TT that year, but Goodwood was not quite the last appearance of the DB3 for 1952. George Abecassis took a 2.6 to Shelsley Walsh for the big end-of-season hill-climb, looking for the sports car record. Ken Wharton (Frazer Nash), already the uncrowned master of Shelsley Walsh, rocketed up the fast, bumpy course in 42.26 seconds. Abecassis nearly beat him, although the DB3 grounded fairly heavily leaving the Esses on its way to 42.28 seconds. Then came the C-type — a car that had not acquired a reputation for controllability on bumpy surfaces — but Peter Walker spoke softly to the works Jaguar and made it fly for him. The result was a new sports car record of 41.14 seconds.

The DB3 had nevertheless ended its season on a high note. Plans for a major updating were already well advanced, and the DB3 was not given any serious publicity to follow up its summer announcement as a production car. Including the works cars, only 10 were in fact built; but I have dwelt on the DB3 here because I think it deserves more attention than it usually gets, by comparison with its successors. After all, it was the very first of the Aston Martin sports-racers.

CHAPTER 5

The DB2-4

Aston Martin's sporting hatchback

Coronation year — 1953 — was the year in which Britons could begin to feel that postwar austerity was beginning to fade away at last.

Early on, 'Pool' petrol was abolished and branded fuels were back for the first time since 1939. Car owners could tune and time their engines to take advantage of the new premium grades, and manufacturers could put up compression ratios.

Although not a totally new concept, the '2+2' came into its own in the UK that year in the form of the Bristol 404, the Jensen 541 and the Aston Martin DB2-4. The last-named was the most significant because it was Britain's first GT hatchback, many years ahead of Jaguar's E-type. The idea of a large accessible luggage area, with the alternative of two occasional rear seats, had never been exploited to this extent before.

More than anyone else, it was former Vauxhall engineer James Stirling who pulled all the Aston Martin and Lagonda projects together at this period. David Brown was based in Yorkshire, as was much of the mechanical work. Feltham remained the headquarters of Brown's car empire, but there were more Midland connections now — Tickfords of Newport Pagnell for Lagonda coachwork (later to be acquired by David Brown, and ultimately to succeed Feltham as headquarters) and Mulliners of Birmingham for the new Aston Martin bodies. It was Stirling who did the spadework, before he emigrated to Canada.

The DB2-4 did not have the purity of line of its predecessor. In adjusting the roofline to help rear accommodation, something was lost. The roundness of the tail was accentuated by the pronounced line of the opening rear panel. But the near-perfect lines of the DB2 would have been hard for anyone to follow and, as a compromise, the DB2-4, with its one-piece curved windscreen, was still an exceptionally good-looking machine by any standards.

The front and centre of the chassis were pure DB2, featuring Claude Hill's square-tube frame and trailing-arm suspension. It took some ingenious redesigning at the rear to make space for the two small seats within the original wheelbase; in fact, these were placed virtually above the rear axle. Finding space for more people and luggage also meant a modification to the fuel tank, and a consequent reduction in capacity from 19 to 17 gallons. The tail of the car had been extended by about 6in, thus adding to the excellent storage space, which was now 50in long with the rear seat-backs folded and nowhere less than 40in wide. Weight was up by 7 per cent, but torque and power were improved to match it.

During the year, the rebodied Lagonda was announced with the 2.9-litre engine, whereas for 1953-54 the Aston Martin retained its 2.6-litre unit. Progress with the development of the 2.9, however, meant that it would soon be in regular production. It was now nearly a decade since the LB6 engine had been announced, and more than five years since the sale of the first Lagonda to be fitted with it.

In the summer of 1954 (after only about 220 had been made) the DB2-4 was given its 2.9-litre engine and a new lease of life — the prelude to several updatings of specification which it would receive during the next few years.

There was no change of model name to go with the bigger power unit, which was fitted to the three cars specially prepared for the 1955 Monte Carlo Rally. Two were for racing team

The introduction in 1953 of the Aston Martin DB2-4 brought the practical advantages of a rear hatch, but at the expense of more bulbous styling. Note the large picture on the wall at Earls Court, which celebrates the outright victory of Peter Collins and Pat Griffith in the TT at Dundrod that year at the wheel of DB3S/4. (Photograph courtesy of *Motor*.)

The cockpit of the 1954 3-litre DB2-4 in which the instrument panel was still mounted centrally and an umbrella handle-type release sufficed for the handbrake (later models had a push-button release alongside the gear lever). (Photograph courtesy of *Motor*.)

Bobby Parkes at the wheel of his 1953 2.6-litre DB2-4 at the start of a test on the 1955 Morecambe National Rally, of which he was to emerge the outright winner. Waiting behind is an HRG sports car.

A former works press car, this DB2-4 Mk II (AM300/1145) was competing at Prescott in 1983. Note the raised roofline and the plated 'brow'.

members Peter Collins and Reg Parnell, but they were not to figure among the prizewinners. Past victors Maurice Gatsonides of Holland and Marcel Becquart of France were paired in the third car and (despite an 8 per cent 'GT' handicap) they looked set for victory until they were caught-out by a secret check. Nevertheless they still came seventh and won a lot of cups. Apart from the 1955 RAC Rally — in which Gatsonides crashed the same car — this was Aston Martin's only works entry in a rally; yet the DB2-4 *could* have become an effective rally car in its day, as this particular 'Monte' and several private owners' successes proved. Bobby Parkes is the best example, with his outright win in the Lancashire Automobile Club's well-known Morecambe National Rally of 1955. (Lyndon Sims' 1956 RAC Rally victory, mentioned earlier, was achieved with an elderly DB2.)

Parkes recalls that, although powerful, his DB2-4 did not have the torque or flexibility required for rallying as the sport became more competitive and arduous. He moved on to an XK 140 (Jaguar's answer to the DB2-4, though even less of a four-seater) but it, too, soon became outdated as a rally car. Bobby Parkes always preferred bigger cars, however, and most of his later rallying was in 3.8-litre Jaguar saloons and Healey 3000s. That was in the early 'Sixties, by which time there was little to recommend the thrashing of exotic Aston Martins between Derbyshire walls or over Alps as a pastime for the privateer.

Two works DB2-4s took part in the 1955 Mille Miglia, but writer-drivers Paul Frère and Tommy Wisdom were unable to prevent clutch failure, despite their experience as marathon runners.

In 1955, too, came the DB2-4's first restyling. In addition to Frank Feeley's classic fastback saloon design, there had been a drophead coupe all along. Now came a third body style, the fixed-head coupe. The first and only DB notchback, its cab bore a distinct family resemblance to that of the 3-litre Lagonda, which was also being bodied by Tickford.

Three views of a rare DB2-4 Mk II (AM300/1282) featuring notchback coupe bodywork with one of its restorers, Simon Moss, at the wheel. Excellent rear and three-quarter vision is a commendable feature.

On the Tickford-built DB2-4, the bonnet was made lighter by moving the shut line up to the top of the front wheelarches, as seen on AM300/1282.

The collective name for this interim series was DB2-4 Mk II. It had a squared-off wing line at the rear, with small (Morris Minor?) lamp units on top. Chromium plate was misused on this series, with a heavy rib running from the front wheelarch to the door jamb to hide the bonnet opening line. Another quirk was the continuation of a plated waist moulding right round the rear deck of the saloon. The worst feature of all was a strangely obtrusive ridge around the top of the windscreen (presumably to make a move from Mulliner to Tickford easier) which spoiled the rooflines of the saloon *and* the fixed-head coupe models.

In the autumn of 1956, David Brown announced a special DB2-4 Mk II roadster with coachwork by Carrozzeria Touring of Milan, to whom three chassis had been supplied, and although this particular project wasn't followed up, it did mark the beginning of an important relationship for the future.

Thankfully, the sleek good looks of the home product, almost on a par with those of the old DB2, were restored to Aston Martin with the arrival in 1957 of the DB2-4 in its Mk III version. Only a handful of Mk III fixed-head coupes were made, but production of the Mk III saloon and drophead increased.

On the Mk III — still a DB2-4 really — the peaked rear wing was altered in shape, slightly, to accommodate a deeper and more modern lamp cluster, like the Humber Hawk's. The 'stuck-on roof' effect of the Mk II was gone, and the frontal aspect was brought up to date with a wider grille and a sculptured bonnetline reminiscent of the DB3S sports-racing machines. The car, which wore its Tickford coachwork badge proudly, looked clean and simple — the true sports saloon car that it was — except when

The beautifully sculptured bonnet lines of the DB2-4 Mk III were a reminder of Frank Feeley's love of curves in general and of the DB3S competition model in particular. This drophead coupe has its headlamps taped ready for a foray on the Silverstone circuit.

painted two-tone, which was fashionable, but didn't suit the Aston Martin at all.

From the Mk II's 140bhp at 5,000rpm, the net power of the much redesigned engine was now up to 162bhp at 5,500rpm, with the option of a twin-exhaust unit giving another 16bhp at the same engine speed. This was supplemented in 1958 by a final 195bhp version called the Special Series, with triple Weber or SU $1\frac{3}{4}$in carburettors and a compression ratio of 8.6:1. To this

The visual differences between the Mk III nearest the camera and the original DB2-4 saloon alongside it can be picked out in this paddock scene at Silverstone. Just visible between them is a DB2-4 Mk II, identifiable by its chromium-plated (and many think unnecessary) waist moulding running right round the tail.

specification, the DB2-4 Mk III became a genuine 120+mph sports saloon.

Aston Martin had long since dispensed with the steering column gear-change option, and the 'umbrella' handbrake was now replaced by a proper 'fly-off' lever. Laycock overdrive had become an option, and the Mk III had Girling disc brakes as standard on the front, though it kept its Alfin drums at the rear. Traditionalists were none too keen on the operation of the servo

Concours racer. Dedicated AMOC members often seem able to combine beauty care with the enjoyment of fast circuit-driving. This lovely car (AM300/ 3/1640) shows the neat vertical rear lamp clusters of the Mk III, the last of the 'DB2' line. Note that the instruments have now been moved to a panel in front of the driver.

Triple SU carburettors adorn the side of the engine of this Special Series Mk III, for which a power output of 180bhp was claimed with a compression ratio of 8.6:1.

Aston Martin chassis have proved a popular platform for specialist coach-builders wishing to display their latest body styling ideas. This open two-seater, first seen in 1956, was the work of Superleggera Touring. (Photograph courtesy of *Motor.*)

assistance under the brake and clutch pedals.

There is no doubt that this Aston Martin had become more comfortable and more sophisticated without losing its sporting character — but after the DB4 arrived in 1958 its days rapidly became numbered. The tautness which went with its good behaviour was less acceptable; times were changing quicker than road surfaces. Steering — now by worm-and-roller as opposed to cam-and-double-roller — did not seem to instill quite the same confidence, either, and it was very heavy at low speeds. On the other hand, the new instrument layout was considerably better, the main dials being in front of the driver instead of centrally positioned.

From 1958, when the DB4 was announced, the old car began to show its age even more, but it kept going right through to the summer of 1959. Thus the DB2 in all its forms had a 10-year life. Despite the problems of manufacture and a very high price, it had sold in considerably larger numbers than the Aston Martins of previous generations.

CHAPTER 6

The DB3S and DBR series

Le Mans winners and Sports Car Champions

In the 'DB2-4 period' from 1953 to 1959, Aston Martin's motor racing efforts — like their sales achievements — rode the swings and roundabouts of victory and defeat. Happily, the decade ended in total glory on a scale that would prove totally unrepeatable.

Often has the story of the DB3S and DBR series of competition cars been told (though there are many anecdotes that have not!) and in a book of this nature, only the highlights can figure. The definitive books by Christopher Nixon and John Wyer are essential reading for any enthusiast, owner, or prospective owner of a DB Aston Martin of the type covered in these pages.

In Chapter 4, the DB3 was seen as a car which never really made the grade — or even achieved lasting fame as a classic sports car — and this has often led to cross-purpose conversations because of the existence of a Mk III which was followed by a DB4 in the road-car sequence.

Clearly, the DB3 was not a born winner, but a successor was already well advanced when the 1953 racing season began. William Watson had to work on it in a rather clandestine way, until Robert Eberan von Eberhorst finally acknowledged its importance. Parallel with this project was one for a V12 competition car — a white elephant which will be popping up from time to time in this chapter.

Prior to Le Mans 1953, works DB3 team cars took part in four events, the first being a two-car presence at Sebring, Florida, in March for the 12-hour race — the first event of the original World Sports Car Championship. Both lost time as a result of collisions due to inexperienced drivers of slower cars. Collins/Duke (DB3/4) had to retire, but Abecassis/Parnell (DB3/5) plugged on to a class victory and second overall behind a big American Cunningham — but on earlier form it was clear that a famous victory for Aston Martin had been lost.

Parnell gave a good account of himself in the Mille Miglia, finishing fifth despite a broken Panhard rod and, later, having to operate the throttle of DB3/3 from the ignition switch. Collins and Abecassis went off-course with broken steering rack mountings. Abecassis (DB3/5) retired, but Collins (DB3/4) struggled on to finish 16th.

The 2.9-litre engine was now fairly well developed, and at the Silverstone May meeting Parnell's DB3/3 had the new car's camshaft profile, 182bhp being quoted (a nominal rise of 22bhp). Ferraris were first and second, but Parnell came third ahead of Collins (DB3/4). DB3/2, driven by Duke — soon to return to motorcycling — broke its clutch.

Whit-Monday, May 25, 1953 (a week before the Coronation) saw the passing of the works DB3 with a win for Dennis Poore from Eric Thompson in the up-to-3-litre sports car race at Thruxton. Poore was also third behind the Stewarts, Jimmy and Ian, in their Ecurie Ecosse C-type Jaguars in the unlimited event.

The DB3S had 'arrived' two days earlier, however, and had beaten the Scottish Jaguars — albeit the previous year's models — on their home ground. That noteworthy occasion was the National Charterhall meeting of May 23, 1953. Three Ecurie Ecosse C-types had made a Jaguar victory look inevitable — and Ian Stewart's did have the legs of everyone until a plug lead came off. Then Reg Parnell in the new Aston Martin (DB3S/1, YMY 307) led, but he was soon passed by Ninian Sanderson

(C-type), who stayed in front, but overcooked the brakes in doing so, made a mistake and gave Parnell the chance he needed. Sanderson was still close at the finish, with a cracked brake drum, but it was Aston Martin's magic moment. The Stewarts, Jimmy and Ian (the latter flying in late pursuit after his pitstop), were to finish third and fourth.

A week later, the Scots came south for their revenge, the final order in the sports car race at Snetterton being Jaguars first and third (Ian and Jimmy Stewart, respectivly), split by the Ferrari of Bobby Baird. Reg Parnell was fourth in the new DB3S, but Le Mans was only a fortnight away; this may have been merely the practice car for the 24-hour race, but this time the usually pugnacious Parnell wasn't going to risk damage from a dust-up.

Those two sprints, at Charterhall and Snetterton, let the British public see the purposeful looks of the new car. Its distinctive curves were the creation of Frank Feeley, the man who had provided such a delightful wardrobe for the 'Bentley' Lagondas of the 'Thirties (and indeed for the postwar ones). Only the mouth-organ grille slats of the early DB3S detracted from the harmony of its lines, although action shots do indicate that taller drivers added to the frontal area by the way they stuck out into the air stream.

The DB3S was considerably more compact than the DB3, as these comparative dimensions reveal:

	DB3	DB3S
Length	13ft 2½in	12ft 9¾in
Width	5ft 1½in	4ft 10¾in
Wheelbase	7ft 9in	7ft 3in
Track	4ft 3in	4ft 1in

Overall weight was down, too — from 17 to 16cwt dry, in round figures.

The 2,922cc version of the 'Bentley' engine was now reliable. Against Eberan's wishes, the bores had been offset to avoid the cost of redesign and recasting, although new connecting rods were necessary. After a first post-mortem and a drawing office rethink, con-rod breakages on the scale of Monaco 1952 were not repeated. The development of this engine was to continue for several years more.

An important feature introduced almost at once by John Wyer and his assistant Brian Clayton was the moving of the rear brakes from inboard to outboard. This set-up was first raced by Parnell and Thompson, who would finish second in the 1953 TT, driving DB3S/2. As early as Le Mans, the new team cars were given updated, lightened versions of the David Brown four-speed gearbox, its bushes replaced by needle-roller bearings.

Watson's chassis improvements still resulted in a pair of tubular 16-gauge chrome-molybdenum side-members connected

The businesslike cockpit of the DB3S. Note the drilled pedals, the rev-counter's telltale registering just over 5,600rpm and the large-diameter steering wheel so typical of the period.

Reg Parnell makes a pit stop with DB3S/2, which he shared with Eric Thompson in the 1953 nine-hours race at Goodwood and helped to drive to victory. Mechanics Jack Sopp (behind the pit counter) and Jack King (in front of the pillar) have completed their tasks, but Parnell has time to clean his screen as the final adjustments are made to his left front wheel.

Peter Collins in the same race and on his way to second place in DB3S/4, which he shared with Pat Griffith. Note the auxiliary lamps for a race which would finish in darkness.

A few DB3S models were fitted with attractive coupe bodywork. This is Graham Whitehead on a very wet day at Silverstone in 1954, when he took DB3S/7 to third place in its class in the *Daily Express* international sports car race behind Roy Salvadori in a similar coupe and Peter Collins in an open DB3S.

by three cross-tubes, with a fabricated scuttle — basically the Eberan Auto-Union principle. The DB3 had suffered from snaky handling and lateral location of the rear axle was altered to prevent this trait. Still a de Dion unit, the rear end now had spiral-bevel instead of hypoid final drive.

Eberan von Eberhorst had relatively little to do with the development of the DB3S, but he did see its debut before he left the company. The German motor industry was getting back into its stride by 1953, and Eberan the academic was needed by his old organization, the Auto-Union. He was a great Anglophile, and he and his family loved the British way of life; but he had not always been treated in a professional manner, and the offer to return home was far too good to refuse. He was sorry to leave Aston Martin Lagonda and, although he was never understood fully, everyone was as sad as he was when he went. Harold Beach, who made the presentation to the great man, verifies this. James Stirling — 'Operations Director' would probably be his most appropriate title — recognized the long-term loss particularly. For John Wyer, however, Eberan's departure would mean a step

After their accidents at Le Mans in 1952, the two works DB3S coupes were rebuilt with open bodywork for 1955 and they dominated the sports car race at Aintree which supported the British Grand Prix that year. Here is Roy Salvadori heading for victory in DB3S/7, with a Lister-Bristol providing him with a cushion in front of his teammates Peter Collins, who would finish in DB3S/6 (car 1), and Reg Parnell, whose DB3S/5 (car 5) was originally built as a road car. (Picture courtesy of *Autosport*.)

up the ladder — although that would take a while. For the time being, David Brown's car group was without technical direction, but extremely active in the competition field, nevertheless.

Le Mans 1953 was a bad international debut for the DB3S team, all three cars failing to finish. Although much better than that of, say, Alfa Romeo, Maserati, or even Ferrari, the Aston Martin finishing rate at Le Mans in the 'Fifties would never again touch the 'five out of five' achieved by the DB2 back in 1951. The DB3S would be second three times, however, before its successor, the DBR1, gave Aston Martin that long-awaited Le Mans victory.

The record of winning marques in the decade 1950 to 1959 reads as follows:

Number of starts		Finishes	Firsts	Seconds
Aston Martin	39	14	1	4
Ferrari	71	17	2	0
Jaguar	40	20	5	3
Mercedes-Benz	6	2	1	1
Talbot-Lago	23	8	1	2

Further body changes were in store for DB3S/7, and this is how the car looked when it was raced in 1956 and 1957 by the works team and how it appears today in the hands of Richard Pilkington. Note the characteristic offset wheel rims.

John Dalton, the first private owner of DB3S/10, shows off the lines of the 'wishbone' car at a 1958 Silverstone club meeting. Note the head fairing on this, the last definitive version of the DB3S.

Roy Salvadori followed up the DBR1's successful first season of racing, in 1957, by driving its logical development, the 3.7-litre DBR2, incorporating a revised chassis, to a convincing victory in the sports car race at Silverstone that September, during the course of which he equalled the sports car lap record.

Back in 1953, however, Aston Martin's new model reaped its rewards elsewhere. Immediately after Le Mans, Reg Parnell drove the DB3S prototype splendidly from scratch to win his heat and the final of the British Empire Trophy, *and* to break the outright lap record for the bumpy Douglas road circuit. In the process, DB3S/1 again defeated the Ecurie Ecosse Jaguars, plus Moss' works car, Hans Ruesch's 4.1-litre Ferrari and a host of Frazer Nashes led by Ken Wharton's, which was second on handicap.

Parnell was very much on form, and he won again for Aston Martin at Silverstone (DB3S/4), Charterhall (DB3S/1) and Goodwood (DB3S/2), where he shared the wheel with Eric Thompson in the nine-hour race (thrown away by Jaguar for the second year running).

Peter Collins and Pat Griffith (DB3S/4) won the TT a fortnight later, the Dundrod race having been revived after a year's lapse. This was when DB3S/2 came second, using the outboard rear brakes which were to become standard. The works Jaguars were let down by faulty gearboxes, but they had not been having it all their own way before that. The DB3S was already proving itself a fine performer on difficult surfaces.

David Brown had wanted to develop a big Lagonda road car on a par with Rolls-Royce-Bentley, as it had been in the 'Thirties. It was to have had self-levelling torsion-bar suspension, a de Dion tube and a V12 engine; Eberan had worked on it for a good two years, but still it wasn't getting very far.

White elephant tales are not as easy to remember as success stories, so the decline and fall of the $4\frac{1}{2}$-litre V12 Lagonda cannot be chronicled completely. Before it was shelved, however, the project came out of captivity in the form of DP115/1, DP115/2 and DP166/1 — three Lagonda-badged prototypes which took part in four races between them. They caused disruption and dismay throughout the DB car empire to the extent that even David Brown himself had to agree to their abandonment. As 12-cylinder cars, they do not belong in this book except in the context of the adverse affect they had — on the Aston Martin racing team in particular. The result was that in 1954 and 1955 the racing programme became far too diverse and complicated.

A win by Collins (DB3S/1) at the 1954 Silverstone Grand Prix meeting could not compensate for another disastrous Le Mans — no finishers again — and little joy elsewhere. Even Dundrod provided no joy, and the Goodwood nine-hour race was cancelled. 1954 had been expensive, too, with the loss of two attractive but aerodynamically unsound DB3S coupes — DB3S/6 and DB3S/7 — at Le Mans, where DB3S/1 was run supercharged to give 240bhp. The regular works DB3S engine was now giving 225bhp, having been modified extensively; it had a redesigned crankshaft and connecting rods, and there were two plugs per cylinder in its new alloy head. As this was proving reliable, supercharging was forgotten.

Avon went through a bad patch at this time, too, but Aston Martin stayed loyal and, after careful study of some of the latest Pirelli racing covers, Avon were back 'on the ball' again.

1955 was brighter except, of course, for Le Mans, which provided no prestige for motor cars or motor racing because of the awful accident which cost the lives of so many spectators. Thankfully, Aston Martin were not involved, and one of their cars — DB3S/6, rebuilt as an open car and driven by Collins and Frère — came an almost unnoticed second. After one try-out with Lockheed in 1954, Girling disc brakes were now being used by Aston Martin — Wyer had wanted discs for a long time — and the sweetest victory of 1955 came in the revived nine-hour race at Goodwood, a circuit notoriously hard on brakes. Here the winners were the mercurial Peter Walker (who had been dropped by Jaguar) and steady Dennis Poore in the other ex-coupe DB3S/7. The DB3S was now more distinctive than ever with a very attractive air intake (better-looking than the original 'chip-fryer') and most unusual offset Borrani wheels with their spoke locating rims protruding beyond the tyres to clear the new discs.

July saw John Wyer's appointment as Technical Director, but he retained control of the racing side and, having already acquired the services of newcomer Tony Brooks, he also managed to snap up Stirling Moss for the 1956 season. If there was a perceptible beginning to Aston Martin's final push for the elusive summit of success in motor racing, this was it; and the respect had to be mutual, for Aston Martin had the reputation of paying as little money as drivers would take. Brooks, Moss and Salvadori (the latter having bought a works DB3S for himself) all had good wins in home internationals, and for the second time a DB3S was runner-up at Le Mans, Moss and Collins hounding the victorious Ecurie Ecosse Jaguar to the end.

Another important mid-'Fifties acquisition, from Austin, was

Endurance racing at its best. Friends, but great rivals, and both former Jaguar team-leaders, Stirling Moss and Mike Hawthorn were driving for Aston Martin and Ferrari, respectively, in 1958 sports car races and were actually contesting the lead when they made simultaneous refuelling stops during the Nurburgring 1,000Kms. However, Hawthorn was still filling his tank when Moss left the pits in DBR/3, which he had been sharing with Jack Brabham, and Stirling went on to score the second of what would become a hat-trick of Aston Martin wins in the German endurance race covering the period 1957 to 1959.

Tony Brooks aboard DBR2/2 at Oulton Park for the 1958 British Empire Trophy race, in which he would finish second to Stirling Moss in DBR2/1. Both cars were fitted with 3.9-litre engines, but later that summer they would be given 4.2-litre power units and sent to the USA for Bob Oker and George Constantine to drive.

Tadek Marek, a talented Polish engineer, who was to be a key man in Wyer's team of technicians. His main job was to create a new engine, but he also did a lot to update the existing one, and several variations appeared. The basic differences are listed in the appendices.

At the end of 1956, John Wyer's job as Technical Director was expanded to that of General Manager. This gave him the opportunity to retain the services of Reg Parnell — by that time Britain's most experienced top-line racing driver — by offering him the job of non-driving Racing Manager. Parnell's nephew Roy had already had three years' experience as a tester and he, with Brian Clayton, formed the nucleus of the Aston Martin racing team in its three best-ever seasons — 1957, 1958 and 1959. Another notable tester was Des O'Dell, famous later for his expert management of the Chrysler/Talbot rally programme.

In 1956, a new car had been designed for Le Mans, to suit 2½-litre prototype regulations introduced as a reaction to the previous year's freak accident. In charge of its design was Edward Cutting. This was the DBR1, fitted initially with a 60-degree twin-plug engine, its stroke reduced from 90 to 76.8mm. The front end was similar to that of the DB3S, but the multi-tube spaceframe was new, as was the five-speed differential-mounted David Brown gearbox with transverse shafts and spur gear final drive. The engine and gearbox were stressed members, and the frame was 60lb lighter than that of the DB3S. At Le Mans, the car had retired with bearing failure quite late in the race, having run as high as fourth.

This promising debut was followed by a couple of good UK race results early in 1957, when Roy Salvadori was twice runner-up to Archie Scott-Brown in the Lister-Jaguar — by now

The 1958 Tourist Trophy at Goodwood was to provide Aston Martin with a 1-2-3 walkover, the joint winners being Tony Brooks and Stirling Moss. Here is Moss pressing one of the fast but ailing Lister-Jaguars. (Photograph courtesy of *Motor*.)

Britain's most competitive vehicle for the XK 3,442cc engine, Jaguar's own lively D-type chassis having become distinctly outclassed in sprint races. Aston Martin, however, had an alloy-block version of the old 83×90mm (2,922cc) twin-plug engine ready to fit into two cars in time for the Spa-Francorchamps sports car race on May 12, and these finished first and second, driven by Brooks (DBR1/2) and Salvadori (DBR1/1),

respectively. A fortnight later, Brooks, driving the same car and partnered by Noel Cunningham-Reid, won the Nurburgring 1,000 Kms outright — a marvellous victory after an arduous race. Soon, the Aston Martin was proving itself to be a world-class competition car, helped by a wide-angle cylinder head to facilitate the use of larger-diameter valves and a redesigned alloy, dry-sump crankcase.

Le Mans 1959 — Aston Martin's finest hour. The D-type Jaguars lost their former reliability when the 3-litre engine limit was imposed, although the former works cars, now raced by Ecurie Ecosse, were still very fast on the Sarthe circuit. Here Roy Salvadori tucks the nose of DBR1/2 in tightly behind Innes Ireland's long-nose D-type, which is destined to retire. Salvadori and Carroll Shelby went on to achieve for Aston Martin the pinnacle it had been striving to reach for nearly a decade — victory at Le Mans.

The 1957 Le Mans 24-hour race regulations provided a brief return to relative freedom, and Wyer responded with a competition version of Aston Martin's new 3.7-litre engine for one of the works entries, despite designer Marek's wish to avoid any racing involvement; it had not been part of his previous experience. This car (the first of two DBR2s, with semi-backbone chassis developed from the 1955 version of the abortive V12 Lagonda) broke its gearbox at Le Mans, but both DBR2s did well at Silverstone in September.

In 1958, Stirling Moss returned to the team from Maserati; Jack Brabham and Tony Brooks assisted him to DBR1 victories in the Nurburgring 1,000 Kms and Goodwood TT races, but at Le Mans (now with a 3-litre limit, like other World Championship sports-car events) the entire works DBR1 team failed to finish. However, the Whiteheads in their old DB3S/6 kept hopes alive for Aston Martin, eventually taking a steady second place.

Le Mans was the only budgeted event in Aston Martin's 1959 racing programme, but that soon changed. Sebring's Alec Ullmann was persuasive, and Aston Martin sent a car, only to

Aston Martin DBR1s are still being kept busy! This is Mike Salmon on the starting grid for an historic race at Silverstone at the wheel of Viscount Downe's famous ex-works car, DBR1/1.

trip-up on its Achilles heel — the transmission. David Brown was never one to do things the easy way, and 1959 saw him launch out briefly into Formula One Grand Prix racing. However, the effort was ill-timed, for a design revolution was occurring. (In 1959, for the first time, a rear-engined lightweight Cooper was to win the World Championship; the Aston Martin was front-engined in the traditional mould, and overweight, and proved uncompetitive with the new breed of lightweights.)

The second round of the Sports Car Championship — the Targa Florio — passed without Aston Martin scoring a point. Then, early in June, came the Nurburgring 1,000 Kms; Stirling Moss was the persuader this time, and Wyer agreed to let old DBR1/1 (now on the 'retired' list) out on the circuit again, with Reg Parnell and two mechanics to run the pit. Moss' chosen co-driver, Jack Fairman, spun off during the race, but he managed to manhandle the car back on to the course unaided, thereby enabling Aston Martin to win this gruelling event for the third year running.

At Le Mans, Moss/Fairman (DBR1/3) set the pace, but broke an inlet valve after 70 laps, but otherwise it was Aston Martin's great year, and almost unbelievable to those involved. It had taken him 10 years, but David Brown had done it! The fierce battle sidelined six Testa Rossa Ferraris and four Jaguar-engined machines, leaving Aston Martin — by now the world's best-handling *and* the fastest long-distance sports-racer — to cross the line first *and* second after 24 hours. Roy Salvadori and Carroll Shelby were the winners in DBR1/2, and Paul Frère and Maurice Trintignant did a fine team job as runners-up with DBR1/4.

Suddenly, with four races gone, Aston Martin had overtaken Porsche in the Championship and was second only to Ferrari — Feltham 16 points, Maranello 18. Moreover, with Venezuela about to be cancelled and only three scores to count, everything now depended upon the outcome of the TT at Goodwood — a proven 'Aston Martin' circuit.

Once again, dangerous refuelling arrangements led to a pit fire in which the leading Aston Martin was gutted! Parnell promptly signalled in the Shelby/Fairman car (DBR1/2); Moss took over, and the Ferraris and Porsches were defeated. Aston Martin had become Britain's first and only World Sports Car Champions. Nothing that followed could ever match the brilliance of that achievement.

Suddenly there were new priorities. The Grand Prix programme hung on into 1960, but the sports car team was disbanded. 1959 had been a justifiably proud year, but the job had been completed. Brown, Wyer and their colleagues knew that Aston Martin must now take advantage of the prestige that had taken so much time and money to acquire. To produce and sell Aston Martin road cars was now, more than ever, the priority. The DB2 was 10 years old and, although it had been updated three times, it was too old-fashioned to justify further manufacture.

Fortunately, its brilliant successor was already gaining rave notices . . .

CHAPTER 7

The DB4, DB5 and DB6

Super Sixes for the 'Sixties

No Aston Martin should ever be referred to as a bread-and-butter model, but all things are relative. Special projects — only some of which saw the light of day, either as fascinating prototypes or ones-off — were always being worked upon behind the scenes of DB's car division.

Even the smallest company needs a staple product, however, and throughout the 'Fifties the DB2 had been developed to fill that role. It had been an exciting decade for British industry emerging from the 'utility' years to set the nation on course for the prosperity and sophistication of the 'Sixties.

British sports cars were still very special animals, but they tended to be rehashed when sales fell. Complete redesigns were rare, and 1957 saw Aston Martin and Jaguar prolonging the youth of existing sports cars with cosmetic treatment which hid the age of the structures beneath. (That was the year in which Lotus set new design standards with the Elite.) While Aston Martin were introducing the DB2-4 Mk III and Jaguar their XK 150 to maintain the interest of devotees, both companies had already built prototypes for completely new machines. Jaguar's E-type, previewed at Le Mans in 1960, would not hit the headlines until March 1961. Aston Martin, on the other hand, succeeded in producing their new masterpiece in time for the London motor show of 1958, merely two years after John Wyer's appointment as General Manager of Aston Martin Lagonda Ltd.

As early as 1955, Tadek Marek (who, like so many Poles, first came to Britain as a member of the allied forces) had begun working on a more powerful successor to the 2.9-litre production engine which he had rejuvenated as an interim measure. Harold Beach, too, had prepared the ground for a new chassis which would have a similar wheelbase to that of the DB2, but be laid out to take two rear seats for people with legs; Beach wanted his new chassis to incorporate a de Dion rear end, but another decade would pass before that went into a production road car (in the DBS).

With his promotion, Wyer became an even more significant figure. Unlike Jaguar, Aston Martin had nothing to protect it from obsolescence. Despite the setback of a disastrous factory fire of February 1957, the compact 2.4 and 3.4 Jaguar saloons were giving the Coventry firm a new string to its bow, whereas the only DB four-door saloon — the 3-litre Lagonda — was on the point of being dropped. Good looks and performance were not enough to offset high price and poor passenger accommodation.

John Wyer felt no attachment or personal loyalty towards the name Lagonda. Much more important to him was to get Aston Martin production out of Yorkshire and into Newport Pagnell, Buckinghamshire, for David Brown now owned the Tickford works there. (Joseph Salmons had been a coachmaker in Victorian times; the company had stayed in the Salmons family for many years, making Tickford bodies for cars. The company had been sold once, but had continued its traditional trade, and coachwork for the 3-litre Lagonda was already being made there when David Brown purchased the company from its current owner, Ian Boswell.) Labour relations and diplomacy were to occupy much of Wyer's time while Newport Pagnell was being expanded to become the car group's main factory.

Suddenly, Tadek Marek's new engine was specified in aluminium. This was no whim; it was a matter of finding a foundry with the facilities available. Marek had designed the

Two views of the beautiful Superleggera-type body of the original DB4, which was announced in Autumn 1958. This car is DB4/544/R and is owned by AMOC registrar Alan Archer.

A trio of sleek DB4 tails without bumpers on the start line at Silverstone for a race in 1983. The car in the centre is a Third Series model, identifiable by the different rear lamp arrangements.

block in cast-iron originally, but he had to acquiesce if production was to become a reality.

There was some rethinking for Harold Beach, too, once the decision to go to Italy for the new car's bodywork had been taken. It had been thought that Pininfarina would do the job, but in the end Touring got the contract. They had made several special bodies for Aston Martins, and Wyer liked their Superleggera construction system, which consisted of aluminium body panelling over a small-diameter steel-tube framework with a rigid platform base; his favourite example was the Alfa Romeo Sprint.

Fortunately, Harold Beach got on well with the Touring designers in Milan, and between them they had a prototype of the DB4 running in July 1957. Frank Feeley, who had styled so many beautiful cars by now, was one of the old team who regarded Newport Pagnell as being 'out in the sticks' — Milton Keynes and the M1 did not exist then — and he decided that he would not move when Feltham was no longer the company's headquarters. His styling had been outstanding, and the new car's shape, though created in Italy, was certainly worthy to succeed it. Truly, it was this car which brought *Gran Turismo* to Britain.

An Aston Martin comes home. This Second Series DB4 was photographed in 1960 at the entry to the Buckinghamshire village which helped to give the car its name. Note the pronounced step in the booted tail, which had replaced the DB2-4's rear hatch. (Photograph courtesy of *Motor*.)

As engineer-in-charge, Harold Beach was rightly proud of the DB4 when it was launched — perhaps a bit earlier than it should have been — his only big disappointment being the temporary discarding of 'his' de Dion rear end because no-one could supply quiet enough final drive units suitable for mounting on the chassis.

The DB4's hasty introduction is reflected in the five distinct versions introduced in as many years. Most important of the early modifications was an increase in oil capacity — from 15 to 17 and, ultimately, to 21 pints. An oil cooler would become optional on the second and third series of DB4s, following a number of bearing failures (as keen owners tried to tour too grandly on Europe's new motorways), and standard for the fourth series. The single-plate clutch would give way to a 9in twin-plate unit. On the whole, and despite its very high cost, the

DB4 was applauded universally as the finest high-performance GT car in Britain.

In May 1959, the organizers of the International Trophy meeting as Silverstone put a Grand Touring car race in the programme for the first time, giving Aston Martin the ideal opportunity to run the forerunner of an even faster version of their powerful new machine — the DB4GT — in which Stirling Moss won virtually as he pleased. Then the car (DP199/1) was fitted with the ex-DBR3 3-litre engine for Le Mans, where it was due to give support to that final, successful, DBR1 works onslaught — but it retired early, its bearings and its race run.

Instantly identifiable by its headlamps set back beneath smooth cowls, this short-wheelbase lightweight had an outstanding power-to-weight ratio, being nearly 200lb lighter than the regular DB4. Moss drove one of the first production

The Series Four version of the DB4, which was introduced in 1961, was distinguished by a different grille, and at this stage the two-door saloon was augmented by this stylish convertible. Compare the much shallower air intake in the bonnet top with that of the original DB4.

DB4GTs (0103) to victory in the Bahamas Speed Week GT race at the end of the year.

There were even lighter cars to come in 1960, however, when international GT racing began to take over from the World Sports Car Championship which Moss' and the DBR1 had just won for Britain. The 3-litre limit had started the rot, and now there was a new and unpopular rule (one of many) which required windscreens to be at least 25cm deep, giving rise to some freakish-looking machines — notably the Tipo 61 and 63 Maseratis. Aston Martin and Lister had already announced their withdrawal as works teams and Ferrari, Maserati and Porsche were left to contest the world series alone — Ferrari taking the title again in 1960 and 1961, after which the World Sports Car Championship was abolished. David Brown decided to stay in Formula One for 1960 — this last year of the 2½-litre formula — but Grands Prix were now being won almost exclusively by cars with the driver ahead of the engine, so that plan was a waste of time.

There was just a handful of super-light DB4GTs, the first of these (chassis 0124) being raced for Tommy Sopwith's Equipe Endeavour by Stirling Moss at Goodwood on Easter Monday, 1960; the car won this closed-car event from a pair of the new

Jaguar 3.8-litre Mark 2 saloons. Jack Sears scored a couple of wins with it soon afterwards.

It was another team, however, which was to put Aston Martin, briefly, on the GT map — John Ogier's Essex Racing Stable. After a gap of two years, the famous Tourist Trophy race had been transferred from Ulster to Goodwood, where it had been won by Aston Martins in 1958 and 1959. For 1960, John Ogier obtained a pair of super-light cars (chassis 0125 and 0151, later registered 18 TVX and 17 TVX, respectively), and entered them for the TT, where the opposition included six Ferrari 250GTs. Moss drove the Dick Wilkins/Rob Walker Ferrari to victory, covering just over 107 laps in the three hours, but little more than a lap behind came the two Aston Martins. Indeed, Salvadori, who had shared best practice time with Moss, led the master briefly before the pit stops began. A puncture for Salvadori and a detached exhaust for Innes Ireland put the Aston Martins out of

sight of the flying Ferrari, but it was a good result even so. Salvadori (0125) was second and Ireland (0151) third, followed by Graham Hill in a very fast Porsche Carrera Abarth, four Ferraris and a horde of Lotus Elites and Porsches.

After this excellent showing, it was thought (just as with the E-type Jaguar two years later, and just as erroneously) that Aston Martin might defeat the Ferrari regularly in GT racing. At Montlhéry, Ireland and Salvadori (0125) came sixth, but up-and-comers Jim Clark and Tony Maggs (0151) retired with engine trouble.

At the 1960 Geneva show one of the delights was a new coupe based on the diminutive twim-cam Alfa Romeo Giulietta. Bertone's curvacious Sprint Speciale version had already been presented; now Zagato showed its gorgeous, taut-lined miniature called the Alfa Romeo SZ.

That autumn, at Earls Court, Zagato showed three beautiful

GT racing arrived in Britain with style when Stirling Moss drove the DB4GT prototype (DP199/1) to victory at Silverstone in May 1959. Note the cowled headlamps, which became the most obvious distinguishing feature from the normal DB4.

silver-grey GT bodies on Alfa Romeo, Bristol and Aston Martin chassis. The latter was so reminiscent of the little Alfa Romeo seen earlier, yet its bulldog stance and DB3S-style grille gave it a very special appearance; beautiful, but all its own. It looked (as John Bolster put it to *Autosport*'s readers) 'fierce beyond belief'. This DB4GT Zagato was the first of 19 such bespoke machines, all covetable and accounted-for in recent years.

Ogier's team remained the mainstay of Aston Martin's competition presence for 1961, when Sir William Lyons stole the Geneva limelight with his new E-type priced at SF 26,700 (undercutting the standard DB4 by SF 17,000). A purposeful Bertone-bodied Aston Martin (built on DB4GT chassis 0201) was simply overshadowed at this show, though it would have made news had the DB4GT Zagato not existed as a dream car already.

Stirling Moss gave the Zagato its race debut, driving the 1960 London show car (chassis 0200) at the Easter Goodwood meeting, but its handling had not been sorted out and Moss had to be content with third place behind Mike Parkes (Ferrari) and Innes Ireland in the 'old' Ogier Aston Martin (0151).

Ireland was fastest in practice for the Oulton Park spring meeting, but it was Graham Hill in the brand-new Jaguar E-type (entered by Sopwith) who kept the Aston Martin back in second place once again — though Ireland did beat Salvadori in another of the sleek Jaguars, a John Coombs entry, and all three of them beat the Ferraris of Jack Sears and Graham Whitehead.

At this stage in the season, Ogier's new Essex Racing Stable DB4GT Zagatos were in preparation for Le Mans, where both retired — as did Kerguen's entry. Then, in July 1961, Australia's Lex Davison gave one of them (0183, registered 2 VEV) a dramatic last-lap victory over the Coombs E-type, driven by Sears, at Aintree's British Grand Prix meeting.

At the TT, the Ferrari-Aston Martin fight went in favour of Maranello once again, Stirling Moss winning from Mike Parkes, both in 250GTs — but Ogier's three Aston Martins came next, and not so very far behind, in the order Roy Salvadori (DB4GT Zagato, 0182, 1 VEV), Jim Clark (DB4GT Zagato, 0183, 2 VEV) and Innes Ireland (DB4GT, 0151, 17 TVX). They were rewarded with the team prize.

Autumn 1961 saw the arrival of a drophead coupe body on the

99

The public announcement of the 3.7-litre DB4GT as a production model came in September 1959. The recessed headlamps and neat grille pattern combined to offer a particularly clean frontal appearance.

The DB4GT's bonnet top removed to expose an impressive sight. With the aid of three twin-choke 45DCOE4 Weber carburettors, dual ignition and a compression ratio of 9:1, the 3.7-litre engine offered 302bhp at 6,000rpm.

The majority of DB4GTs were sold as two-seaters, with useful additional luggage space behind, although a few were equipped with small rear seats suitable for children. (Photograph courtesy of *Motor*.)

DB4, and it was followed soon afterwards by a new Vantage-specification model with high compression ratio, larger valves and triple SU HD8 carburettors. This, in effect, succeeded the various short-chassis DB4GTs, of which only 100 would be built, including several racing or experimental models, not all of which can be described as 'genuine DB4'. These project cars travelled immensely quickly at Le Mans in 1962 and 1963, but never actually finished. Only one of them ever had a really good win, and that was 0194/DP 214 with which Roy Salvadori defeated Mike Parkes (Ferrari GTO) in the 1963 Coppa Inter-Europa at Monza. To beat a Ferrari on its home ground provided a moment of joy; but it was the thin end of the wedge. By bringing in their beautiful GTO as another version of their already virtually invincible 250GT, Ferrari had ensured that GT racing was

Ferrari property. The magnificent DB4GT had had its day, as far as international racing went.

An Alvis opportunity

While this final fling at motor racing was taking place, John Wyer had been concentrating on the job of directing the car business on David Brown's behalf, and one of his plans to improve the production situation was to enter into co-operation with Alvis of Coventry — still independent and, like Aston Martin, struggling.

John Parkes (father of the late racing driver Mike Parkes) was in charge at Alvis' Holyhead Road plant, and he and Wyer got well down the road towards a merger. The two marques seemed to them to be compatible, Alvis being considered for engine and chassis manufacture, AML for bodies and assembly. Those

A Jaguar-versus-Aston Martin battle developing at Oulton Park during the 1962 Spring National meeting. Robin Sturgess and his E-type are being chased by George Pitt in DB4GT/0125/R, one of the ex-Essex Racing Stable lightweight cars.

Beautifully brutal — the DB4GT Zagato, first seen at Earls Court in October 1960 and looking every inch a race-winner. Note the two power bulges in the top of the bodywork to provide adequate clearance above the engine.

103

Although 25 years old, this car (DB4GT/0181/L) still shows the tautness of Zagato's brilliant styling at its best and emphasizes the restoration standards set by today's Aston Martin specialists — in this case Richard Williams. Bumpers were not fitted originally, but no one should complain about the neat and unobtrusive way in which this tail is protected.

combined facilities might well have worked for the good of both.

No Lagondas had been made for some four years when, to Wyer's chagrin, David Brown insisted on going ahead with production of a lurking project — the Rapide. This name had been reserved for certain exotic Lagondas in the past, including the 1936-37 LG45 when restyled as a cad's sporting confection by Frank Feeley for his boss, Dick Watney.

Based upon the DB4 in general concept, the new Rapide was exotic, too, with fine smooth lines by Touring. Unfortunately, the detail work around the paired lamps and the three front grilles gave it an unfinished look, which reflected its general state. The Rapide had an enlarged Marek engine, bored out from square to oversquare (96×92mm) dimensions, giving a capacity of 3,995cc. It breathed through two twin-choke Solex carburettors to the tune of 236bhp at 5,000rpm — more than

adequate to propel this big car along smartly. It had disc brakes and — like the racing Aston Martins, but not the production cars — Beach's beloved de Dion rear suspension. Automatic transmission was standard.

Launched in Autumn 1961, virtually at the same time as Jaguar's Mark 10, the Rapide seemed doomed. Desultory output averaged little more than one car a month until a total of 55 had been made. Even at the astronomical £5,000 asking price, no reasonable return for such a dubious investment can be imagined. In 1963, a DB4 grille was applied experimentally, but the lamps still did not look quite right.

By the mid-'Sixties, the 4-litre Rapide — the last six-cylinder Lagonda — was gone. Perhaps it had served a purpose in that it had kept the name alive, and (Sir) David Brown would have a beautiful four-door Towns-styled DBS-fronted V8 Lagonda (see

The last chassis of the series (DB4GT/0201/L) was exhibited at both the Geneva and Turin motor shows in 1961 with this graceful coachwork by Bertone, who named the design 'Jet'.

next chapter) for his own use in 1969. Under subsequent management, the project would be revived with single-headlamp body mouldings *à la* AM Vantage/V8 and a horseshoe-shaped central motif to distinguish it from the standard Aston Martin. Seven, only, would be built — all with V8 engines. Today's V8 Lagonda (another Towns shape) is still the world's most eye-catching four-door saloon — but more a plaything of sheiks than a serious competitor for Rolls-Royce.

Back in the early 'Sixties, the introduction of the Rapide against his advice, plus its adverse effect upon his discussions with Alvis, altered Wyer's relationship with Brown, and in June 1963 John Wyer resigned after more than 13 years with the company — most of them as its most influential day-to-day employee. He returned to the arena he loved best for a further eight years and guided the paths of Ford, Gulf and Porsche into the new era of international sports-car racing. His departure meant the end of racing for Aston Martin (although the team itself had really disbanded in 1960) and it meant the end of Feltham as administrative headquarters. Without the racing and

car manufacture on site, all that was left now was a service workshop. The change of emphasis had come several years earlier, when DB4 production had begun at Newport Pagnell, which now also became Head Office.

The fifth series DB4 was more roomy than its predecessors; it had become a very fine car. What might have been the sixth series was given the 96×92mm (3,995cc) engine and the title DB5. This was by no means overstretching an engine which, in competition form, had gone as far as 98×92mm (4,164cc).

Introduced in the autumn of 1963, the DB5 is, in the view of many enthusiasts, the ultimate Aston Martin of the Italianate era. The big punchy engine had three SU carburettors as standard, but the Vantage version on this occasion was a triple-Weber unit — a logical option, since the DB4GT was no longer being offered.

The DB5 began life with a four-speed in-house gearbox, overdrive being optional, but later, a ZF five-speed became standard and the modern practice of fitting a diaphragm clutch was now adopted. Twin fuel fillers are probably the most obvious

The Lagonda Rapide of 1961 was the first production model to be given Aston Martin Lagonda's 4-litre engine. Based largely on the DB4 in its construction, the car featured a de Dion rear end. In theory, it was a supercar *par excellence,* but in practice it could not be be made economically or consistently well, and was a factor in John Wyer's decision to leave the David Brown Organisation.

Two distinctly different styles of dashboard were tried for the revived Rapide, which was to be the last six-cylinder model to bear the Lagonda name.

Differences between the various factory-built models became quite difficult to identify from 1961, when the DB4 Vantage was announced. This variation anticipated the DB5 in having triple SU carburettors and GT-type headlamp cowls while retaining the standard four-seater wheelbase. This is the works prototype car (DB4/951/R).

The Kerguen/'Franc' Aston Martin Zagato (DB4GT/0180/L) leading a typical group of prototype and GT cars away from the Le Mans start in 1962. No two Zagato Aston Martins seemed to be exactly alike, and this example had a distinctly shallower grille.

Probably the most famous Zagato Aston Martin of them all, this car (DB4GT/0183/R) has been owned by Roger Hart for many years. Here it is in its Essex Racing Stable days, crossing Aintree's Melling Road on the occasion of its famous last-lap victory over Jack Sears' Jaguar E-type in the race supporting the 1961 British Grand Prix. Surely this is the slowing-down lap — or did Lex Davison really drive with his elbow out? (Photograph courtesy of *Autocar*.)

distinguishing features — although some late DB4s also have these. The progression from DB4 to DB5 was very much a running change, as is so often the case in specialist car manufacture. A wider market was catered for in the DB5, with Borg-Warner automatic transmission being available at extra cost on soft-engined cars, and a nicely contoured steel hardtop provided for drophead owners to hang in the garage until winter. Harold Radford, famous for the Bentley Mk VI Countryman conversion of some years earlier, made several DB5s and their successors into estate cars. One of the best-known names of the

era — James Bond — became closely associated with that of Aston Martin, and several DB5s were specially modified to undertake impossible tasks for Ian Fleming's hero, as played by Sean Connery.

In 1965, it was decided to give the occupants still more room, and nearly 4in was added to the wheelbase. The overall length went up a couple of inches to 15ft 2in, and the tail was totally redesigned with a spoiler effect derived from the DP project car. This car, the DB6 (in saloon form) also had totally reshaped rear quarter-lights, not unlike those of the DB4GT Zagato. Front

The last three competition Aston Martins (DP212, 214 and 215) were built with the 4-litre prototype regulations in mind. Here is John Wyer alongside DP212, talking to Graham Hill, who was to share the car with Richie Ginther in the 1962 Le Mans 24-hour race.

DP212 went extremely well at Le Mans in 1962 before retiring during the seventh hour with oil pressure trouble. Here is Graham Hill leading the Ferrari 330LM of Olivier Gendebien and Phil Hill, which was destined to win the race.

quarter-lights were re-introduced for the first time since the Carrozzeria Touring design of body had been adopted.

Touring was now going out of business (although they did get in a couple of special Aston Martins, regarded as DBS prototypes, before the shop shut), and for some inexplicable reason the DB6 did not continue to be made on the Italian company's tooling, which had produced such rigid structures. Harold Beach still recalls the quality problems which came to light at this stage, such as doors that dropped as they had not done before.

On the plus side, dial-a-ride Selectaride shock absorbers were fitted as standard, and new instruments were easier to read. Other recognition features were a more steeply raked windscreen and an extra lower grille for the essential oil cooler. Air conditioning was an optional extra, but automatic transmission could be specified at the same price as the standard ZF five-speed gearbox. Power-assisted steering was also available now.

The DB6 was soon overshadowed by the DBS but, nevertheless, it overlapped with it for several years. Drophead coupes were not called DB6, but Volante. To complicate matters, early Volantes were, in effect, DB5s carried over. A Mk 2 version of the DB6 was announced as late as summer 1969, distinguished

DP212 was to be joined by DP214 and DP215 for 1963, but DP214 was the only one of the trio to achieve success that year when Roy Salvadori won the Coppa Inter-Europa at Monza. Here, appropriately numbered, is DP215, in which Phil Hill had been timed at 197mph down the Mulsanne straight during Le Mans practice.

by slightly contoured wheelarches to accommodate broader wheels and tyres. Besides the usual triple-carburettor choice (SUs or Webers), AE Brico fuel injection was offered — but it was not a success.

The DB6 was a fine performer, and very comprehensively equipped. It was not quite a 150mph car — the only road-going Aston Martin to achieve that figure was the light DB4GT — but even in its old age it was regarded as a very grand tourer indeed.

Test reports, however, began to indicate that it was not as comfortable or convenient as it should have been, and in America, especially, the random instrument layout and poor seat-belt anchorages were noted. The age of legislation was approaching with a rapidity which Aston Martin could not match. In fact no application was made to certify the DB6 in the USA, so it was inevitable that it petered out. Indeed, it is perhaps surprising that it continued until well into 1970, even

An Aston Martin DB5, which was meticulously restored at Jack Moss' Four Ashes Garage in Stratford-upon-Avon during 1982 and 1983. The cowled headlamps, first seen on the DB4GT and then on Vantage models, became a standard DB5 fitment.

The front-hinged bonnet of the DB5 opens wide to facilitate top-end maintenance. With these triple SU 2in carburettors, the 4-litre engine should produce 282bhp at 5,500rpm in standard form.

The attractive dashboard of the DB5, with instruments neatly grouped around the steering column. Approximately 900 of the 1,063 DB5s built were supplied with saloon bodywork, although 12 of these were subsequently converted into estate cars.

The elegant lines of the DB5 convertible, of which some 125 examples were produced, are seen to particular advantage when the hood is lowered and the door windows remain raised. Substantial overriders offer vital protection at the front without detracting from the car's appearance.

overlapping with the exciting new DBS V8.

1967 was probably the DB6's worst year for sales and, because it was his business, David Brown slashed prices on a scale that no unprotected company could have contemplated. This moved enough cars to keep production going and staff employed and, together with the arrival of the new DBS, helped put off the evil day.

In 1968, 'DB' became *Sir* David Brown — the success of his

other companies, it must be said, being as much to do with the accolade as his beautiful cars of Royal patronage. Then, early in 1972, just over a year after the demise of the DB6, Sir David sold Aston Martin Lagonda. Meantime, there had been no DB7. The DB6 had been succeeded by the DBS, and the 'DB' identity would soon disappear — even on the last of those great six-cylinder cars, none of which would have existed if it had not been for David Brown's whim, 25 years earlier.

The name 'Volante' was applied to convertibles on late DB5 as well as on DB6 chassis. They are identifiable by their split bumpers, an additional oil cooler intake and a DB6-style tail. However, buyers of these cars, in particular, should be sure about exactly which model they are examining; this is where the Aston Martin Owners Club Register is so useful.

There is little difficulty in identifying a DB6 saloon by its upswept tail treatment. The car in the foreground is a DB5 convertible, but saloon models are very similar up to wing height, as illustrated on an earlier page.

The Harold Radford conversion on the DB5, which turned the two-door saloon into a sleek estate car. The idea was also carried forward to the DB6, but the upswept rear end of that model detracted from its appearance after conversion.

One of the last DB6s (DB6/Mk2FI/4257/R), dating from 1970 and featuring flared wheelarches. Split bumpers had now become standard equipment. *Car & Driver* described the DB6 as 'a hard-riding, hard-steering reminder of the good old days, with luxury and lots of Old World Charm — like Rocky Graziano in a Coldstream Guard's uniform'.

One concession to an easier life. This DB6 has been equipped with the optional automatic transmission in place of the standard five-speed manual gearbox. The dashboard layout of the DB6 is similar to that of the DB5, although some of the instruments were given improved markings.

The cockpit of a 1965 DB6 Vantage revealing fully adjustable leather covered seats with well-rounded backrests and generously proportioned cushions. Door windows were electrically operated, but quarter-lights were still adjusted by means of a knurled wheel.

The AE-Brico fuel-injected version of the DB6 Mk 2, which unfortunately was never developed successfully.

This is the engine of DB6/Mk2F1/4257/R, which was converted from fuel injection to authentic Weber carburation during its rebuild by Jack Moss at Four Ashes Garage.

CHAPTER 8

The DBS and beyond

The last of the six-cylinder cars

In 1966, William Towns pricked up his ears. An interesting snippet had filtered through on the motor industry's grapevine. Aston Martin Lagonda were scouting for a Chief Body Engineer as well as a Seat Designer; the DB6 was in need of replacement, fabulous though it still looked. Expensive cars, no matter how sporting, also had to be comfortable these days.

Two years had passed since the last Lagonda had been built. Of 55 made, only eight had been exported. Its development had been inadequate, *and* probably too late, for this was not the first break in Lagonda continuity. The marque had not sustained its special appeal sufficiently to bring back regular customers who had had to defect when there was no Lagonda to buy. (Bristol have never lost continuity and, whatever the in-house difficulties, enough customers have kept returning for the gunwales to remain fairly dry.) Despite the lapse, David Brown still wanted to market a Lagonda as well as an Aston Martin.

William Towns had joined the Rootes Group as a pupil in 1954 and had stayed on in their styling department after his training. From 1963 he had been with Rover during one of their most creative periods. Neither of the Aston Martin job opportunities was related directly to styling, and this was the field in which Towns was most determined to progress. An admirer of Bill Mitchell and his GM styling team, Towns worked not only with flair and inventiveness, but also with an eye to production practicality. He decided to accept the seat-design job, while Cyril Honey — ex-Pressed Steel Fisher and ex-Hindusthan(!) — was appointed Chief Body Engineer.

In addition to the collapse of Carrozzeria Touring, the autumn 1966 credit squeeze did no good for Aston Martin's Italian connection. Project Engineer John Howarth was brought back from Milan to Newport Pagnell, together with two short-wheelbase prototype show cars with neat Superleggera bodies; after the shows were over, these machines were retained for testing.

Towns continued to design seats, but soon began drawing body shapes, too. He knew that David Brown wanted a two-door and a four-door in his next new range of cars. He had also noted how the styling of Bristol cars had lost its way when the 404 had been stretched into the 405; the 405 may have been more practical, but the neat, clean look was gone. Much more recently, he had also seen the dubious effect of adding 9in to Jaguar's E type to make a 2+2 of it.

The Towns theory was that first you should create your 'long' model, thus establishing a satisfactory length-to-width relationship, then adapt your GT model from it. This way, he believes, you can be sure of a stubby, powerful-looking shape — an effect epitomized by the DB4GT Zagato body (though that would not have been achieved by the same means). From the outset, Towns worked on long and short-wheelbase models, without much notice being taken.

By October 1966, the economic crisis was hitting Aston Martin hard. From well into double figures, sales had plummeted to three or four cars a week, and the London motor show gave no boost to hopes of any improvement in the immediate future. Meanwhile, Towns had made sure that David Brown had seen his ideas. 'Very nice', (DB had said) '— but now, would Mr Towns please go back to his seats?' Then the word came down the line. Towns was to go ahead and turn his drawings into reality — but he was to shelve the

The first Touring-bodied prototype (266/1/R), which is generally regarded as the starting point for the DBS, seen on a road in Italy in 1966.

The second Touring-bodied car (266/2/L), which was shown at Earls Court in 1966 and was subsequently bought by Tom Leake.

Lagonda and concentrate on the GT model. He insisted on having a clay oven, and he got one at once.

What might have been the DB7 and DB8 became known as the DBS — as awkward a name as any before it, but what a marvellous shape!

The existing DB6 was 182in long and 66in wide. Towns' Lagonda design had measured 192in by 72in. Shorter by 1ft, but retaining an overall width of 6ft, the DBS in its definitive form certainly possessed those chunky dimensions of Towns' theory. Sir David Brown has said since that, too late, it was discovered that the jigs had been made too wide and that it would have been too costly and time-consuming to alter them. What seems much more likely is that, too late, he had had a change of heart over the agreed width; but there was nothing he could do anyway. Harold Beach makes it clear that the DBS's width was determined by that of the new V8 engine in relation to the necessary front wheel movement — a much more logical explanation.

Bert Thickpenny, a craftsman of the old Salmons days — and,

The definitive DBS shape, but the car is still in pre-production prototype form. Both the split front bumper and the air extractor grilles behind the side windows were to be discarded from the final specification.

The Aston Martin DBS in its production form. Although the car was designed for the forthcoming V8 engine, it would be two years before the new power unit was ready for production, and so when the DBS was unveiled at the end of 1967 it was offered with the DB6's Tadek Marek-designed 4-litre six-cylinder engine with a choice of triple SU carburettors or, in Vantage form, triple Webers.

incidentally, the probable shaper of the Tickford-built Healey 100 prototype — was responsible for the body skin lines of the new car. With only a short time for the project, expediency had to be combined with artistry in the creation of the DBS, and the basis was therefore a widened version of the existing DB6 chassis. It had been thought that Superleggera-type tubing would be incorporated, as in the two smaller Touring prototypes, but Cyril Honey's experience led him to opt for a substructure in the form of steel pressings — which, to a great extent, were to account for the car's excessive weight. Wider wheels and tyres, and Beach's

long dreamed-of de Dion tube at the rear, helped, too, to make the DBS the first 1½-ton Aston Martin ever.

The combination of 'Coke bottle' effect with clear definition of line made the DBS distinctive in the extreme, and it was tooled-up quickly. William Towns remembers going out on test in the prototype with Development Engineer Michael Loasby in July 1967, and it appeared in public, alongside the DB6, that autumn. And that is really the beginning of the end of this story, for the DBS was designed around Tadek Marek's last masterpiece — an oversquare 90-degree V8 engine, closely related to his old 'six'

The dashboard layout of the early DBS with the seven instrument dials arranged in a straight line ahead of the wood-rimmed steering wheel. Note that, unlike most earlier DB models with right-hand drive, the windscreen wipers on the DBS park to the right.

Long doors which open wide are a feature of the roomy DBS. Note the novel release handle, also the generous bolstering at shoulder level and the integral armrest incorporated into the door trim.

The chassis structure of the DBS: the method of construction chosen, using steel panelling, was similar to that of the preceding DB4, 5 and 6 models, although at one time consideration had been given to using a tubular framework.

with two camshafts per cylinder bank. In early form it had teething problems highlighted by a half-hearted 1967 racing programme for which the new unit was fitted into Lola's T70 structure. By the time the DBS was ready, however, the V8 was not; Marek had in fact retired by the time the V8 engine was being offered for sale.

The DBS V8 was announced in September 1969, but it did not mark the end of the 'six' altogether. The Volante Mk 2 and DB6 Mk 2 lived on into 1970, while the relatively sluggish DBS was made in ever-decreasing numbers until 1973. The last 70 were not in fact called DBS, but were given the old engine designation Vantage. Why? — because 'DB' himself was no longer at the helm.

1972 was a sad year for the company. Enthusiast though he was, Sir David Brown could not ignore the profitability of his Group as a whole. He had invested in an almost doubling of tractor production, only to be caught out by a world sales slump.

On the car side, it had proved impossible to keep up with the safety and emission regulations for the USA, and worldwide sales were down to a trickle. How could he justify living with the losses of his car business? Interest in the marque was maintained in a couple of V8-engined show cars — by Ogle and by Trickett — while Sir David himself ran the prototype Towns-styled Lagonda which had finally seen the light of day with a V8 engine in 1969. Towns, who had left the company to go freelance in 1968, showed his concept of a scaled-down DBS (still using the V8 engine) to Brown, who said he wanted to build it. But it was too late. Nowadays, whenever Sir David Brown is quizzed about his sale of Aston Martin Lagonda Ltd, the phrase 'liquidity problems' always crops up.

The firm became a subsidiary of Company Developments Ltd, of Birmingham, chaired by William Willson, who is better remembered in Newport Pagnell today for chopping down the fine avenue of trees leading to nearby Tickford Abbey than for

The last of the 'sixes' — the Aston Martin Vantage of 1972 and 1973, by which time the car had been deprived of its 'DB' identity. Nevertheless, there was no disguising the fact that this was a car born of a David Brown heritage.

putting new life into Aston Martin. In fairness, the impact of the late-1973 fuel crisis was felt by the whole motor industry. Nevertheless, the apparent suddenness with which the entire Aston Martin workforce was declared redundant at the end of the following year still took enthusiasts by surprise.

The British Government could step in and help Rolls-Royce, but not, apparently, Aston Martin. Two North Americans, George Minden and Peter Sprague, set a new company in motion in mid-1975, and they were joined by a British businessman and enthusiast, Alan Curtis, who ran it for four difficult years during which the quality, production and selling problems of the by now all-V8 Aston Martin range were tackled with vigour. What sapped *this* management's energy most was the time it took to develop the spectacular and futuristic new V8 Lagonda as we know it today. That we do know it today is due to the arrival on the scene of Victor Gauntlett, early in 1981. Like so many of his predecessors,

he is a true motoring enthusiast and, $2\frac{1}{2}$ years later, he was still Executive Chairman of Aston Martin Lagonda, despite the sale by his own company, Pace Petroleum, of its Newport Pagnell interests in July 1983. This meant that ownership was now shared between Automotive Investments (owners of Aston Martin Lagonda's importing and distribution company in North America) and CH Industrials — the British firm which had shared financial responsibility for AML with Pace since New Year 1981. Victor Gauntlett said then that he believed strongly in Aston Martin's future.

Apart from helping Pace after a difficult year (as it was for the whole of industry in 1982), Gauntlett pointed out that the new deal would 'bind Aston Martin more closely to those responsible for sales in the US, its most important single market'.

The stalwarts of Newport Pagnell are used to walking a tightrope, and will probably keep walking it. There have, after

The very last 'DB'? William Towns drew this proposal shortly before Sir David Brown sold Aston Martin Lagonda Ltd. Later, in an interview with journalist Wilson McComb, Sir David said that it would have been 'smaller and lighter, with a front engine and rear transmission'. However, the scaled-down DBS was not to be.

all, been many changes — and the life-support machine has almost been turned off on several occasions. Nevertheless, the great names of Aston Martin and Lagonda continue to bring prestige to Britain now that a healthy export market has been re-established.

Over a decade has passed since the last of the six-cylinder cars left the works. (Its customer, in fact, was the well-known former MG racer Dick Jacobs.) It was the 70th Vantage version of what had started out as the DBS. Those 70 cars were the hangover from a very special era which had produced some very special machines to delight the discerning and wealthy motorist.

In his 80th year, Sir David Brown could look back from his retirement home on the Riviera knowing that his quarter-century in charge of Aston Martin had built it into a Le Mans-winning marque of world fame (and out-of-this-world pricing) which in turn had made the tasks of his successors seem a little less daunting.

In the end, though, this epic of survival is a tribute to the employees and customers who stayed loyal when all seemed to be lost.

CHAPTER 9

Ownership and maintenance

Clubs, specialists and parts availability

Unlike most cars covered by the *Collector's Guide* series so far, the six-cylinder Aston Martins and Lagondas have a complex technical history. All were, in effect, hand-built (to use a well-worn euphemism) and as such could be subject to variations of detail specification at any time.

Fortunately, the Aston Martin Lagonda movement is highly organized. The clubs operate as clubs should do — promoting and maintaining enthusiasm for the two marques, and involving themselves fully in the interests of their members. They organize events on their own, and in conjunction with other clubs; and of course they provide services. Each club has its technical and parts specialists for individual models but, for the enthusiast starting from scratch, it is best to contact the club secretaries for the latest information. In 1984 these are:

Mrs Valerie May	Mr James Whyman
The Lagonda Club	Aston Martin Owners Club
68 Savill Road,	Ltd
Lindfield	Burtons Lane
Haywards Heath and	Chalfont St Giles
West Sussex	Buckinghamshire
(Tel: 0444-414674)	(Tel: 02404-4742)

The Lagonda Club was formed in October 1951 as an amalgamation of the Lagonda Car Club and the 2-litre Lagonda Register. Membership is around the 700 mark and the annual subscription at the time of writing is £10, after a joining fee of £5. Publications include a quarterly 'glossy' and a monthly newsletter.

The AMOC dates back to 1935 and is also famous for its wide range of activities — especially for the excellence of its race meetings and the enthusiasm of participants. It, too, in addition to its monthly news sheet, has a splendid A4-sized monthly magazine edited by Brian Joscelyne, who has been living and breathing Aston Martins, driving them with pleasure and in anger *and* writing about them with authority, for over 20 years.

Since Aston Martin Lagonda Ltd was restored to life by Victor Gauntlett and his colleagues in the early 'Eighties, a full line of official distributors and dealers has been appointed. These include specific service-only dealers. All are expert specialists, or they would not hold the appointment, but I make no apology for having singled out several of them for special mention in the context of this book.

Aston Service Dorset Ltd, of Longham, on the A348 near Bournemouth, is the focal point for the earlier six-cylinder Aston Martins and Lagondas, and it is a rare day when other specialists are not on the telephone to The Captain (Ivan Forshaw) or one of his sons, who have fully justified the trust placed in them by the manufacturer.

Ivan Forshaw had been a Lagonda enthusiast in the 'Thirties. The war (in which he had been a transport officer) left him in poor health, but his enthusiasm was undimmed and his inclination towards the Staines marque led him back to it in the purchase of a 2-litre saloon. His main activity — to keep Lagondas on the road — thrived while Lagonda as a company went downhill. From about 1950 — shortly after the David Brown acquisition — Forshaw's Lagonda specialization moved on to a true business footing, and has not looked back. An Aston Martin connection followed quite naturally.

In 1970 or thereabouts (when David Brown was coming under pressure to dispose of his car interests) the old Aston Martin Lagonda company let it be known that it would no longer cope with the supply of spares for its earlier products. All relevant parts up to the DB5 were put in stillages, and tenders were invited on a 'per stillage' basis. Captain Forshaw realized the danger of letting such a stock become split up, and was able to negotiate both total purchase of tooling, drawings and records, *and* the manufacturing rights.

Aston Service is run by Captain Forshaw, together with his son Richard. His other son, Roger, is an accountant by profession, and guides the financial side. The extent of their six-cylinder model parts responsibility is from DB2 and Lagonda 2.6 to DB4 and Rapide, but of course their capabilities take their operations right up to current models. (The Newport Pagnell factory caters for DB5 and later spares.) Few owners of cars within those ranges — made in the 15-year period from 1949 to 1964 — do not have good reason to be thankful for Aston Service. When a part is no longer available it is usually manufactured 'in house', by other good engineering companies, or sometimes even by the original supplier. In the case of the latter, the continued investment can be a problem. For example, Hepolite is cited as a helpful company, but one which, nevertheless, is not prepared to make special pistons of one type in batches of less than 250.

A visit to Aston Service (preferably by appointment, as with most specialists) is rewarded not only by the visual reassurance that an early DB Aston Martin should never be off the road for long, but by the sight of several fine DB competition models owned by the Forshaws. Most specialists are dedicated, but some are more dedicated than others. The Forshaws look at you askance if you ask them when they take holidays.

Although not within the scope of this book, the servicing of the four-cylinder prewar Aston Martin should be mentioned in passing, for there is one firm which operates exclusively for this rare breed — Morntane Engineering Ltd, of College Yard, Highgate Road, London NW5 1NX. Tel: 01-485 2376.

Probably the best-known of London-based DB specialists is Richard Williams, whose premises 'underneath the arches' at 31-35 Padfield Road, London SE5, have been an Aston Martin marque mecca for many years. Williams began his Aston Martin apprenticeship in the early 'Sixties, when the company was still actively involved in racing, and race preparation of famous cars is his particular forte. He looks after the cars of AMOC President Viscount Downe, and one of his 'trademarks' is an attractive works-style metallic paint finish (actually Ford Forest Green) for race-prepared DB4s.

Today's official service dealers for the London area (see the end-of-chapter list for details) are Hyde Vale Garage and Ian Mason Aston Services. The former is run by V8-racer Raymond Taft and tends to be associated with the more recent models, but late DB models are very much at home there, too. Ian Mason, like Richard Williams, is a former employee of Feltham and Newport Pagnell, having joined as an apprentice in the late 'Fifties. Such directly applied experience is of rare value to the private owner.

A third specialist with a factory background is Peter Austen Smith, whose apprenticeship began at Feltham back in 1957. His personal engineering experience of the cars when they were new has stood him in good stead. His firm, PAS-Mobile, occupies the old fire station at Olney, not very far from Newport Pagnell. Tel: 0234-711502.

Noteworthy listed DB people near the centre of Britain are Robin Hamilton, of Burton-on-Trent, and Chapman-Spooner, of Walsall. Hamilton is most famous for his Nimrod and other V8 racing exploits, but his company offers comprehensive work on all DB models — especially those from 1959 onwards — including alloy and steel panel work, loom-making and all types of rebuilding and service work.

Andrew Chapman and John Spooner offer complete mechanical rebuilds of all types. Chapman was an Aston Martin man, so here is another case of experience being put to good use. His knowledge is comprehensive on 'Bentley' *and* 'Marek' engines; gearbox and transmission work are undertaken, too, and there is a bonus in that John Spooner runs a precision machine shop.

For early DB work, however, no-one in the Midlands is better known than Jack Moss and his son Simon, who run the Four Ashes Garage at Pathlow, just north of Stratford-upon-Avon on the A34. They concentrate on the DB2, DB2-4 and DB4, stocking new and secondhand spares for them and undertaking any kind of work. Jack Moss, like Ivan Forshaw, was a Lagonda enthusiast, so here again the Lagonda element is not forgotten.

On the whole, services such as those already mentioned are carried out to a very high standard, complete and authentic in every way, and priced accordingly. Sometimes cars are even better than new afterwards. It may seem to cost the earth to re-platform a DB4, 5 or 6, but when it is done it should last another 20 years; and where bodies once leaked, some licence is taken by the experts to prevent rabid rot for the second time around. Where wiring harnesses passed through structures, for example, Aston Martin draughtsmen were not always required to guarantee a seal against water and dirt — nor were they alone!

Labour time being what it is, the degree of near-perfection has to be balanced against cost. Those who race or use their cars in all weathers probably get the most pleasure from ownership, and there are several firms who cater more for the 'user' than for the complete restorer.

Vic Bass Engineering Ltd (which is associated with CV Shapecraft in Northampton — Tel: 0604-495177) is a good example. The Bass address in London is Arch 63, Queens Circus, Battersea, SW8 4NB (01-720 4565).

Britain from the Midlands southwards is well served, but when this book was being compiled, there was no true Aston Martin Lagonda specialist advertising his services or recommended for the north or Scotland apart from today's works-appointed agents.

The following list of services is not comprehensive, but it is a starting point. I apologise if I have made any serious omissions, but, surely, any specialist soon becomes well-known locally — and the owner will soon find him, form an opinion, and pass it on. That is where the clubs are such an asset, and why, in the end, there is no substitute for club membership.

LONDON

Aston Martin (Sales) Ltd 33 Sloane Street London SW1X 9NR (01-235 8888)	Distributor. Up-to-date information on official representation.
Hyde Vale Garage Ltd Hyde Vale Greenwich, London SE10 8HP (01-692 2822/8122)	Official service and spares agents.
Ian Mason Aston Services Ltd 139a Freston Rd (formerly Latimer Rd) Bayswater, London W10 (01-727 1944)	Official service and spares agents.
R.S. Williams 35 Padfield Road (off Coldharbour Lane) London SE5 (01-733 1062/0659)	Run by former factory man.

SOUTHERN ENGLAND

Aston Service Dorset Ltd 73 Ringwood Road Longham, Wimborne, Dorset (0202-574727)	Official service and spares agents, notably 'DB' AM & L cars pre-DB5.
H.W. Motors Ltd New Zealand Avenue Walton-on-Thames Surrey, KT12 1AT (09322-20404)	Official distributor, formerly associated with DB's son-in-law, George Abecassis. Frank Nagle now in charge of service.
Safir Engineering Ltd Unit T815, Brooklands Industrial Park Weybridge, Surrey (0932-55266)	Formerly Maybridge Engineering of Staines.

Other official UK service dealers in South:
Hursley Garage, Winchester, Hants
Woodmancote Garage, Dursley, Glos
Marshalsea Motors, Taunton, Somerset
St Helier Garages, Jersey
St Peter Port Garages, Guernsey

MIDLANDS

Aston Martin Lagonda Ltd Tickford Street Newport Pagnell Bucks, MK16 9AN (0908-610620; Telex 82341)	Factory and service information and post-DB4 spares. Parts Manager Michael Adams.

Robin Hamilton Group Fauld, Tutbury Burton-on-Trent Staffs, DE13 9HR (0283-813939, Telex 34337)	Official distributor, behind Nimrod and other race projects.
Marshall (Cambridge) Ltd Cherry Hinton Road Cambridge, CB1 4AX (0223-249211)	Official distributor.
Chapman Spooner Ltd Unit 7, Middlemore Lane Aldridge, Walsall, WS9 8SP (0922-51896)	Official service and spares agents — and specialists.
Four Ashes Garage Ltd Birmingham Road, Pathlow near Stratford-upon-Avon (0789-66851)	Specialists in all models covered in this book, notably the earlier cars.

Other official UK service dealers in Central area:
A.V.J. Developments, Pershore
Stratton Motor Company, Long Stratton, Norwich
Donaldson & Evans, Sale, Greater Manchester
Arnold G. Wilson, Leeds

SCOTLAND & NORTHERN ENGLAND

Victor Wilson Ltd Haymarket Terrace Edinburgh and at Dunkeld Road, Perth (0738-38300)	Official distributor (and service dealer at Perth).

Reg Vardy Ltd Stoneygate Houghton-le-Spring Tyne and Wear, DH4 4NJ (0783-842842)	No longer listed as current agent, but long-running advertiser in club magazines.

The foregoing is a fairly arbitrary selection, based on known or official services. At any time, the Aston Martin Owners Club and the Lagonda Club are the best initial sources of UK information.

The revived company has appointed (or reappointed) a number of overseas distributors, and a list of these can be obtained from the works or from Aston Martin Sales in London. In addition, there is a fairly long list of USA stockists and servicing dealers. The best places for up-to-date information are Aston Martin Lagonda Inc, 342 West Putnam Avenue, Greenwich, Connecticut 06830 (tel: 203-629 8830) where former UK racing driver Peter Gaydon is in charge of operations, or the company's West Coast address: 629 North La Cienega Boulevard, Los Angeles, California 90069 (tel: 213-854 3536).

As the world's leading 'DB' spares stockists, with special responsibilities for the pre-DB5s, the Forshaw family of Aston Service in the Dorset village of Longham (tel: 0202-574727) provide the key to successful and happy ownership. They deal direct with owners in all parts of the globe and, as the name of the firm implies, service and restore vehicles on their own premises. They even have their own North American parts supplier: Kenneth Boyd, 1035 Bollinger Canyon, Moraga, California 94556 — probably *the* most useful address for any Transatlantic 'DB' owner or discoverer.(Tel: 415-376 6633)

Aston Martin and Lagonda introduction dates

ASTON MARTIN

Summer 1949	DB2	Prototype first seen (Le Mans)
Spring 1950	DB2	Official announcement of saloon
Autumn 1950	DB2	Drophead coupe introduced
Winter 1950-51	DB2	First Vantage engine option
Autumn 1951	DB3	Prototype first seen (TT, Dundrod)
Summer 1952	DB3	2.9-litre version first seen (Monaco)
Summer 1953	DB3S	Prototype first seen (Monza test; then Charterhall)
Autumn 1953	DB2-4	Saloon and drophead coupe announced
Summer 1954	DB2-4	2.9-litre version introduced
Autumn 1954	DB3S	Production model offered
Autumn 1955	DB2-4	Mk II introduced (saloon, drophead and fixed-head coupes)
Summer 1956	DBR1	Prototype 2.5-litre first seen (Le Mans)
Spring 1957	DB2-4	Mk III introduced (saloon, drophead and fixed head coupes)
Summer 1957	DBR1	2.9-litre version first raced (Spa, May)
Summer 1957	DBR2	First raced (Le Mans)
Summer 1958	DBR3	Raced once only (Silverstone, May)
Autumn 1958	DB4	First series saloon announced
Summer 1959	DB4GT	Prototype first seen (Silverstone, May; then Le Mans)
Autumn 1959	DB4GT	Official announcement
Winter 1959-60	DB4	Second series saloon introduced
Autumn 1960	DB4GT	Zagato-bodied version offered
Spring 1961	DB4	Third series saloon introduced
Autumn 1961	DB4	Fourth series saloon and drophead coupe introduced
Summer 1962	DP212	Special competition coupe first seen (Le Mans)
Autumn 1962	DB4	Fifth series introduced
Spring 1963	DP214	Special competition coupe first seen (Le Mans practice)
Summer 1963	DP215	Special competition coupe first seen (Le Mans)
Autumn 1963	DB5	Saloon and drophead coupe (hardtop optional) introduced
Autumn 1965	DB5/6	First of several estate cars
Autumn 1965	DB6	Saloon announced
Autumn 1965	Volante	Short-chassis (DB5-based) drophead coupe
Autumn 1966	Volante	Mk 1 (DB6-based) drophead coupe
Autumn 1966	DBS	DBSC (prototypes bodied by Carrozzeria Touring)
Autumn 1967	DBS	Definitive model announced
Summer 1969	DB6	Mk 2 saloon announced (continued to Nov 1970)
Summer 1969	Volante	Mk 2, drophead coupe version of DB6 Mk 2
Spring 1972	AM Vantage	New version of DBS, but not designated 'DB' due to new company ownership
Summer 1973	AM Vantage	Six-cylinder Aston Martin discontinued

LAGONDA

Autumn 1945	2½-Litre	Press announcement of new 2.6-litre cars
Autumn 1946	2½-Litre	Further details in press
Winter 1946-47	2½-Litre	First full descriptions (prior to 'DB' acquisition)
Autumn 1949	2½-Litre	First road tests (drophead coupe and four-door saloon)
Autumn 1952	2½-L, Mk II	Announcement of updated model
Autumn 1953	3-Litre	2.9-litre Tickford two-door saloon and drophead coupe introduced
Autumn 1954	3-Litre	Four-door saloon introduced
Autumn 1956	3-L, Mk II	Updated four-door saloon and drophead coupe (two-door saloon phased-out)
Winter 1957-58	3-L, Mk II	2.9-litre Lagondas phased-out
Autumn 1961	Rapide	4-litre DB4-based four-door saloon introduced
Autumn 1965	Rapide	Six-cylinder Lagonda discontinued

APPENDIX B

Aston Martin specifications

DB2 (1949 to 1953)

Engine: 6-cyl, twin overhead camshaft, Bentley-designed, 60-degree valve angle, hemispherical combustion chambers, 78 × 90mm, 2,580cc, CR 6.5:1, twin SU 1½in carburettors, 105bhp at 5,000rpm. (More powerful versions became available later, as with most 'DB' Aston Martins — see engines table.)

Transmission: Standard and close-ratio 4-speed gearbox alternatives. Final-drive ratio 3.77:1 standard (3 alternatives). Borg and Beck single-dry-plate clutch, Salisbury hypoid differential.

Chassis: Rectangular-tube frame based on Atom/DB1. Ifs by coil springs, trailing links and torsion bar (transverse); live rear axle with coil springs, trailing links and Panhard rod. Worm-and-roller steering, 12in drum brakes, Girling hydraulic operation; 6.00 × 16in tyres.

Bodywork: 2-seater saloon body with one-piece bonnet. Split-bench seating; central instrumentation. Drophead coupe added October 1950. Various early grille changes, 2-piece screen.

Dimensions: Wheelbase 8ft 3in (252cm); length 13ft 6½in (413cm); width 5ft 5in (165cm). Approx weight 2,480lb (1,125kg).

Prices: Saloon £1,920 in 1950, £2,720 in 1952. Drophead coupe £2,040 in 1950, £2,880 in 1952. Chassis (no Purchase Tax) £850.

DB2-4 (1953 to 1955)

Engine: Initially as DB2 except now developing 125bhp at 5,000rpm. Replaced within first year by engine with 83 × 90mm, 2,922cc, CR 8.2:1, twin SU 1¾in carburettors, 140bhp at 5,000rpm.

Chassis: Modified at rear to permit fitting of 2 small seats, fuel capacity reduced from 19 to 17 gallons.

Bodywork: 2+2 hatchback saloon and drophead coupe bodies, one-piece screen, new rear roofline, higher headlamps, better bumpers.

Dimensions: Length 14ft 1½in (431cm). Approx weight 2,650lb (1,202kg).

Prices: Saloon £2,730 in 1954. Drophead coupe £2,910 in 1954.

DB2-4 Mk II (1955 to 1957)

Similar to 2.9-litre DB2-4 except:

Bodywork: Better seats and handbrake moved from facia to floor. 2+2 hatchback and new notchback (permanent hardtop) now built by Tickford instead of Mulliner. New rear wing line, lower side panels no longer hinge with bonnet, clean lines interrupted by chromium-plated finishers and raised roof. Drophead coupe still offered, but few made.

Dimensions: Length 14ft 3½in (436cm). Approx weight 2,690lb (1,220kg).

Prices: Saloon £3,080 in 1956 (later reduced to £2,880). Drophead coupe £3,300 in 1956. Fixedhead coupe £3,080. in 1956.

DB Mk III (1957 to 1959)

Not to be confused with DB3, the Mk III was a further derivation of the DB2-4 with the following changes:

Engine: Cylinder liners top-seating; crankcase, crankshaft and manifolds all new. Several high-performance versions offered based on DB3S racing experience (see engines table). Special camshafts, twin exhausts and triple Weber carburettors available.

Transmission: Hydraulic assistance for clutch. Laycock de Normanville overdrive available as extra. Borg-Warner automatic transmission available with lower-powered engines only.

Chassis: Front disc brakes introduced; hydraulic assistance for brakes.

Bodywork: Appearance improved by cleaning up roofline and reducing chromium plate; rear lamps much tidier and rear quarter-lights openable; bonnet nicely redesigned in DB3S style. Interior changes included new instrument layout and use of steering-column control stalks. Mostly built as hatchbacks, but some drophead and fixedhead coupes.

DB4 First Series (1958 to 1960)

Engine: 6-cyl, twin overhead camshaft, Marek-designed, 80-degree valve angle, all-alloy, 92 × 92mm, 3,670cc, CR 8.25:1, twin SU 2in carburettors, 236bhp at 5,500rpm. (See engines table for variations.) Oil cooler extra.

Transmission: 4-speed gearbox with 3.54:1 Salisbury hypoid final drive.

Chassis: Composite platform and tube frame (Superleggera) structure. Ifs by coil springs, wishbones and anti-roll bar; live rear axle with coil springs, trailing links and Watt link. Rack-and-pinion steering, disc brakes all round, 6.00 × 16in tyres.

Bodywork: 4-seater close-coupled 2-door saloon body designed by Carrozzeria Touring to Aston Martin requirements but built in UK. Rear-hinged bonnet. (Note: DB4GT models listed separately.)

Dimensions: Wheelbase 8ft 2in (249cm); length 14ft 9in (450cm); width 5ft 6in (168cm). Approx weight 3,000lb (1,361kg).

Price: £3,980 in late 1958.

DB4 Second Series (1960 to 1961)

As first series cars except:
Overdrive available (3.77:1 final drive); improved front brake calipers; oil sump capacity increased from 15 to 17 pints; front-hinged bonnet. Price: £3,970 in late 1960.

DB4 Third Series (1961)

As second series cars except:
Detail improvements including rear lamps now under 3 separate covers on each side.

DB4 Fourth Series (1961 to 1962)

As third series cars except:
Saloon now joined by drophead coupe; less obtrusive bonnet air intake; slight changes to grille and rear lamps (now countersunk); oil cooler now standard; overdrive optional; Vantage and GT engines offered with cowled-headlamp body similar to DB4GT; twin-plate in place of single-plate clutch; 3.31:1 final drive ratio standard (3.54 and 3.77:1 still offered, the latter for overdrive cars). Prices: DB4 £3,880 in 1962. Vantage £4,060 in 1962.

DB4 Fifth Series (1962 to 1963)

As fourth series cars except:
Extra length and cab height for additional passenger space and other detail changes; most cars with Vantage engine and GT headlamp treatment (drophead coupes did not follow this specification consistently); 3 cars supplied with automatic transmission; detachable hardtop offered for drophead coupe. Length: 15ft 0in (457cm).
Prices: DB4 £3,990 in 1963. Vantage GT £4,170 in 1963. Drophead coupe £4,400 in 1963. Extras: overdrive £88; automatic transmission £315; hardtop £200.

DB4GT (1959 to 1963)

Engine: 6-cyl, twin overhead camshaft, Marek-designed, 80-degree valve angle, 92 × 92mm, 3,670cc, CR 9:1, 12-plug head, triple twin-choke 45DCO Weber carburettors, 302bhp at 6,000rpm.
Transmission: 4-speed close-ratio DB all-synchromesh gearbox. Choice of 4.09, 3.77, 3.54, 3.31 and 2.93:1 final-drive ratios.
Bodywork: The majority of this short series of 100 chassis looked similar to the DB4, but both wheelbase and overall length were shorter and the body was in lighter-gauge alloy. Instant identity comes from cowled headlamps and twin filler caps (total fuel capacity 30 gallons). Superleggera saloon bodies normally had only 2 seats, but several were fitted with small rear seats.
Dimensions: Wheelbase 7ft 9in (236cm); length 14ft 3½in (436cm); width 5ft 6in (168cm). Approx weight 2,800lb (1,270kg).
Prices: £4,530 in 1960, £4,670 in 1961 and £4,680 in 1962.

DB4GT Lightweight (1959 to 1961)

Five competition DB4GT models were made, 3 being raced by the works and by Essex Racing Stable (see text).

DB4GT Zagato (1960 to 1963)

Altogether, 19 ultra-light Zagato-bodied cars were built on the DB4GT chassis, some for road use and some for racing; none was identical to another in every detail. Typical power output was 314bhp at 6,000rpm with a CR of 9.7:1 (see text).
Dimensions: Wheelbase 7ft 9in (236cm); length 14ft 0in (427cm); width 5ft 5½in (166cm). Approx weight 2,700lb (1,225kg).
Price: £5,470 in 1962.

DP214 (1962 to 1963)

Designated Project 214, 2 chassis (DB4GT 0194 and 0195) were specially prepared by the works for racing in 1963. DP212 and DP215 were individual cars of the same period with little structural similarity to the DB4GT. All 4 cars had special coupe bodywork (see text) with styling features adopted on the DB6.

DB5 (1963 to 1965)

Derived from DB4 series cars with the following changes:
Engine: 96 × 92mm, 3,995cc, CR 8.9:1, triple SU 2in carburettors, 282bhp at 5,500rpm (Vantage version with triple Weber carburettors, 314bhp at 5,750rpm). These 2 specifications were to remain basically unchanged throughout the remaining life of the Marek 6-cyl engine.
Other changes: Wheels now 6.70 × 15in. Detail body changes including identifying boot badge. Saloon and drophead coupe models supplemented by a few Harold Radford estate cars. Automatic transmission and hardtop still listed as options, likewise overdrive until DB gearbox replaced by ZF 5-speed. Approx weight: 3,200lb (1,452kg).
Prices: DB5 £4,250 in 1964. Drophead coupe £4,570 in 1964.

DB6 Mk 1 (1965 to 1969)

A major update with items like air conditioning, power-assisted steering and more up-to-date automatic transmission optional. Better instruments and 5-speed ZF gearbox now standard. Bodywork with squared-off tail forming spoiler. Saloon bodywork (see Volante below) except for handful of Radford estate cars. Split bumpers an identification feature. Automatic or manual transmission offered at same price.
Dimensions: Wheelbase 8ft 6in (259cm); length 15ft 2in (462cm). Approx weight 3,250lb (1,475kg).
Prices: Saloon £5,090 in 1966, £4,070 in 1967, £4,500 in 1968 and £4,830 in 1969.

Volante (1965 to 1966)

In order to use up the last DB5 chassis, a few drophead coupes were

made in 1965-66 using DB6-type bumpers. They retained the rear-end style of the earlier model.
Dimensions: Wheelbase 8ft 2in (249cm); length 15ft 0in (457cm).
Price: £5,000 in 1965.

Volante Mk 1 (1966 to 1969)
This was truly the DB6 drophead coupe, with DB6 styling and an electric motor for operating the top.
Dimensions: Wheelbase 8ft 6in (259cm); length 15ft 2in (462cm).
Approx weight 3,280lb (1,488kg).
Prices: £5,590 in 1966, £4,580 in 1967 and £5,060 in 1968.

Volante Mk 2 (1969 to 1970)
Last of the DB drophead coupes and really a DB6 Mk 2 (see below).
Prices: £5,420 in 1969 and £6,090 in 1970.

DB6 Mk 2 (1969 to 1970)
Final saloon of the type which ran for over a decade and incorporating a number of features from the DBS which it, and the Volante Mk 2 above, overlapped for some 3 years. Engine options included the experimental use of AE Brico fuel injection. Identifiable by extended wheelarches necessary to cover wheels with 6in rims and 8.15 × 15in tyres. Approx weight 3,300lb (1,497kg). Prices: £4,800 in 1969 and £5,500 in 1970.

DBS (1967 to 1972)
Engine: 6-cyl, twin overhead camshaft, Marek-designed, 80-degree valve angle, all-alloy, 96 × 92mm, 3,995cc, CR 8.9:1, triple SU carburettors, 282bhp at 5,500rpm, or optional at same price CR 9.4:1, triple Weber carburettors, 325bhp at 5,750rpm.
Transmission: 5-speed ZF gearbox or Borg-Warner automatic transmission at same price, limited-slip differential standard.
Chassis: Ifs similar to DB4; de Dion rear axle with trailing links, Watt linkage, coil springs and Selectaride adjustable shock absorbers (also used on some other models).
Bodywork: First 2 prototype bodies built by Touring. Production alloy 4-seater saloon bodies built in-house at Newport Pagnell to William Towns design on widened steel platform. Four headlamps built in.

AM Vantage (1972 to 1973)
Mechanically similar and a DBS by any other name. Identifiable by 2 instead of DBS's 4 headlamps and a return to DB3S style of grille. These cars were designed to be made with the 5.3-litre V8 engine and in that form were still being made more than a decade later.
Price: £6,950 in 1972.

APPENDIX C

Lagonda specifications

2½-Litre (1948 to 1952)
Engine: 6-cyl, twin overhead camshaft, Bentley-designed, 60-degree* valve angle, hemispherical combustion chambers, 78 × 90mm, 2,580cc, CR 6.5:1, twin SU 1½in carburettors, 105bhp at 5,000rpm.
Transmission: Initially specified with Cotal electric gearbox but no Cotal-equipped cars sold. Alternative 4-speed DB gearbox became standard. Final-drive ratio 4.56:1, hypoid bevel differential mounted on frame, Borg and Beck single-dry-plate clutch.
Chassis: Deep crucifrom frame with parallel outriggers to assist body mounting. Ifs by coil springs and wishbones; irs with torsion bars; rack-and-pinion steering; 12in front drum brakes, 11in inboard rear drum brakes; 6.00 × 16in tyres.
Bodywork: Four-door saloon and 2-door, full 4-seater drophead coupe.
Dimensions: Wheelbase 9ft 6in (290cm); length 15ft 8in (478cm); width 5ft 8in (173cm). Approx weight 3,400lb (1,543kg).
Prices: Saloon £3,110 in 1949. Drophead coupe £3,420 in 1949.
*Original Lagonda description quotes valve angle as 62 degrees.

2½-Litre Mk II (1952 to 1953)
Detail improvements including more interior space. Vantage engine fitted giving 125bhp at 5,000rpm. Four-door saloon only. Jackall hydraulic jacking. Approx weight 3,500lb (1,588kg).
Price: £3,000 in 1952.

3-Litre (1953 to 1956)
Mechanically similar apart from larger engine, 83 × 90mm, 2,922cc, CR 8.2:1, 140bhp at 5,000rpm. This was the first use of the 2.9-litre engine in a series production model. Chassis design as 2½-Litre with Jackall

hydraulic jacking.

Bodywork: Completely new 2-door saloon and drophead coupe bodies and 4-door saloon added in 1954.

Dimensions: Wheelbase 9ft 6in (290cm); length 16ft 4in (498cm); width 5ft 9½in (177cm). Approx weight 3,500lb (1,588kg).

Prices: Saloon (4-door) £3,900 in 1956. Drophead coupe £4,500 in 1956.

3-Litre Series 2 (1956 to 1957)

Few changes, but range rationalized to 4-door saloon, although 5 drophead coupes were also made to Series 2 specification. Approx weight 3,750lb (1,701kg).

Prices: Saloon reduced to £3,000 and drophead coupe to £3,380 for

1956 motor show.

Rapide (1961 to 1964)

New 4-door saloon based on DB4 mechanical specification, including disc brakes and de Dion rear end. Powered by 3,995cc engine with 2 twin-choke Solex carburettors, 236bhp at 5,000rpm. This was the first use of the 4-litre engine in a series production model. The last 6-cyl Lagonda and only 55 examples made.

Dimensions: Wheelbase 9ft 6in (290cm); length 16ft 3½in (497cm); width 5ft 9½in (177cm). Approx weight 3,780lb (1,715kg).

Price: £4,950.

APPENDIX D

Chassis numbers and production records: Aston Martin six-cylinder GT cars, 1949 to 1973

Production summary

DB2, DB2-4 and variants (1949-59)	1,725
DB3 and DB3S (see note) (1951-56)	(10)*
DB4, DB4GT and variants (1958-63)	1,212
DB5, Volante swb and variants (1963-66)	1,063
DB6, Volante lwb and variants (1965-70)	1,755
DBS, AM Vantage and variants (1967-73)	899
TOTAL SIX-CYLINDER GT ASTON MARTINS	6,654

*NOTE: These 10 hardtop DB3/DB3S cars are not included in the 'GT' total.

NOTE: The 'DB' terminology did not begin at any identifiable stage. Retrospectively, most of the 16 2-litre 4-cylinder cars made between 1948 and 1950 are known as 'DB1'. Their chassis numbers were LMA/48/1 (the 1948 Spa 24hrs race-winner) and AMC/48/1 to AMC/50/15. The first numbers represented the year (up to and including 1950 only).

The first DB2 prototypes also had the 4-cylinder Claude Hill engine represented by 'A' for Aston Martin in the chassis number. The 6-cylinder W. O. Bentley engine was represented by 'L' for Lagonda. (Who is to say whether the 'LM' originally stood for Lionel Martin or Le Mans?)

DB2 (1949 to 1953)

LMA/49/1	(UMC 64, converted from 4 to 6-cylinder engine)
LMA/49/2	(UMC 65, 4-cylinder)
LML/49/3	(UMC 66, probably the second 6-cylinder Aston Martin)
LML/49/4	(UMC 272, probably the first 6-cylinder Aston Martin)
LML/50/5	(VMG 606, converted from 4 to 6-cylinder engine)
LML/50/6	(production prototype)
LML/50/7	(VMF 63, now Forshaw collection)
LML/50/8	(VMF 64, now The Hon Gerald Lascelles)
LML/50/9	(VMF 65, now Nigel Mann)
LML/50/10	(VMF 37, David Brown's prototype drophead)
LML/50/11 to LML/50/220	(production series)
LML/50/222 to LML/50/406	(production series)
LML/50/X1 to LML/50/X5	(production series)

TOTAL DB2 — 409 including about 49 drophead coupes.

DB2-4 (retrospectively Mk I) (1953 to 1955)

LML/50/221	(prototype and press car)
LML/501	(prototype and demonstration car)
LML/502 to LML/1065	(production series)

TOTAL DB2-4 — 566 including 1 fixed-head coupe (LML5/5 for David

Brown and then Peter Collins) and approximately 75 drophead coupes.

DB2-4 Mk II (1955 to 1957)
AM300/1101 (prototype)
AM300/1102 to AM300/1299 (production series)
TOTAL DB2-4 Mk II — 199 including 37 fixed head coupes and approximately 25 drophead coupes.

DB2-4 Mk III (1957 to 1959)
AM300/3A/1300 (prototype with discs all round)
AM/300/3A/1301 (works demonstration car)
AM300/3/1302 to AM300/3/1850 (production series)
TOTAL DB2-4 Mk III — 551 including 6 fixed-head coupes and approximately 50 drophead coupes (the latter speculative).

DB3 and DB3S (1951 to 1956)
Five of each of these 2 competition types were, at some stage, fitted with GT-style bodywork, namely: DB3/1, DB3/2, DB3/3, DB3/5, DB3/7, DB3S/6, DB3S/7, DB3S/113, DB3S/119 and DB3S/120 (see SPORTS/RACING car appendix).

DB4 (1958 to 1963)
DP114/2 (Experimental car with DB4 front suspension)
DP184/1 (First prototype of DB4)
DP184/2 (Second prototype: Lyndon Sims rally car)
DB4/101 to DB4/249 (First series, saloon)
DB4/250 to DB4/600 (Second series, saloon)
DB4/601 to DB4/765 (Third series, saloon)
DB4/766 to DB4/950 (Fourth series, saloon)
DB4/951 to DB4/995 (Fourth series, Vantage saloon)
(DB4/996 to DB4/1000) (Not used)
DB4/1001 to DB4/1050 (Fifth series, saloon)
DB4C/1051 to DB4C/1080 (Fourth series, drophead coupe)
DB4C/1081 to DB4C/1110 (Fifth series, drophead coupe)
DB4/1111 to DB4/1165 (Fifth series, Vantage saloon)
DB4C/1166 to DB4C/1175 (Fifth series, drophead coupe)
DB4/1176 to DB4/1215 (Fifth series, Vantage saloon)
TOTAL DB4 — 1,113 including 70 drophead coupes and 3 automatic transmission models (DB4 1016, 1037 and 1197). DB4C/1173 was the only drophead coupe to have a GT engine and therefore qualify for the designation Vantage in the DB4 drophead category.

DB4GT (1959 to 1963)
DP199/1 (Prototype, Silverstone winner 1959, etc)
DP212/1 (Special competition car, 1962, with many modified DB4GT components; see text)
DP215/1 (The last works 6-cylinder competition car, 1963, originally

mooted as a V8; see text)
DB4GT/0101 to DB4GT/0166 (Regular DB4GT)
DB4GT/0167 (Experimental lightweight chassis)
DB4GT/0168 to DB4GT/0175 (Regular DB4GT)
DB4GT/0176 to DB4GT/0190 (DB4GT Zagato)
DB4GT/0191 (Project DP209, lightweight Zagato)
(DB4GT/0192) (Not used)
DB4GT/0193 (Project DP209, lightweight Zagato)
DB4GT/0194 and DB4GT/0195 (1963 racing project DP214)
(DB4GT/0196 to DB4GT/0198) (Not used)
DB4GT/0199 (Zagato)
DB4GT/0200 (Original Zagato 1960 show car)
DB4GT/0201 (Bertone-bodied 1961 show car)
TOTAL DB4GT — 100 comprising 74 regular saloons, 19 Zagato-bodied cars, 1 Bertone-bodied car and 6 experimental/racing cars.

DB5 and short-chassis Volante (1963 to 1966)
DP216/1 (Late DB4 Vantage, transmogrified into 1963 DB5 show car, then into *Goldfinger* film car)
DB5C/1251 to DB5C/1300 (DB5 drophead coupe)
DB5/1301 to DB5/1450 (DB5 saloon)
DB5/1451 (project DP217, *Autocar* test car)
DB5/1452 to DB5/1500 (DB5 saloon)
DB5C/1501 to DB5C/1525 (DB5 drophead coupe)
DB5/1526 to DB5/1900 (DB5 saloon)
DB5C/1901 to DB5C/1925 (DB5 drophead coupe)
DB5/1926 to DB5/2100 (DB5 saloon)
DB5C/2101 to DB5C/2125 (DB5 drophead coupe)
DB5/2126 to DB5/2275 (DB5 saloon)
DBVC/2301 to DBVC/2337 (Volante short chassis, a restyled version of the DB5 drophead coupe, overlapping with DB6)
TOTAL DB5 (including Volante swb) — 1,063 comprising 1 prototype, 888 DB5 saloons, 125 DB5 drophead coupes, *12 DB5 estate cars and 37 Volante swb drophead coupes. *Harold Radford estate car conversions from *saloon* chassis sequence, as shown above.

DB6 and Volante (1965 to 1970)
DB6/MP/219/1 (Experimental, de Dion rear)
001/D/P (Experimental, de Dion rear, DB5 with V8 engine, then DB6 engine)
DB6/2351 to DB6/3599 (DB6 Mk 1 saloon)
DBVC/3600 to DBVC/3739 (Volante Mk 1 drophead coupe)
DB6/4001 to DB6/4081 (DB6 Mk 1 saloon)
DB6 MK2/4101 to DB6 MK2/4345 (DB6 Mk 2 saloon)
DB6 MK2VC/3751 to DB6 MK2VC/3788 (Volante Mk 2 drophead coupe)
TOTAL DB6 (including Volante lwb) — 1,755 comprising 2 experimental cars, 1,325 DB6 Mk 1 saloons, 140 Volante Mk 1

drophead coupes, *5 DB6 Mk 1 estate cars, 245 DB6 Mk 2 saloons and 38 Volante Mk 2 drophead coupes. *Harold Radford estate car conversions from saloon chassis sequence.

DBS and AM Vantage (1967 to 1973)
266/1 and 266/2 (Modified DB6s with prototype bodywork by Touring)
DBS/5001 (Production prototype)
DBS/5002 (V8 development car)

DBS/5003 to DBS/5071 (Production series)
DBS/5072 (V8 prototype)
DBS/5073 to DBS/5174 (Production series)
DBS/5175 (V8 special engine from Lola-Aston Martin Le Mans car)
DBS/5176 to DBS/5829 (Production series)
AM/6001 to AM/6070 ('post-DB' production series)
TOTAL DBS 6-cyl (including AM Vantage) — 899 comprising 3 prototypes, 823 saloons, 3 Harold Radford estate cars and 70 AM Vantage saloons.

APPENDIX E

Production engine identification

Prefix	Compression	BHP at RPM	Carburation	Remarks
LB6A/B	6.5:1	105 at 5,000	2 SU (1½in)	DB2/Lagonda 2½-Litre
LB6E	7.5:1	116 at 5,000	2 SU (1¾in)	Bigger manifolds and valves
LB6V	8.2:1	125 at 5,000	2 SU (1¾in)	First Vantage engine
VB6B/E	8.2:1	125 at 5,000	2 SU (1¾in)	2,580cc fitted to most late DB2s and early DB2-4s
VB6J	8.2:1	140 at 5,000	2 SU (1¾in)	DB2-4/Lagonda 3-Litre
VB6J/L	8.2:1	165 at 5,500	2 SU (1¾in)	High-lift cams, special series; bigger valves
DP101	(Numbering used for DB3 and DB3S works cars)			
VB6K	8.7:1	180 at 5,500	3 Weber	Production DB3S, cast-iron head
DBA	8.2:1	162 at 5,500	2 SU	New designation for updated engine (standard in DB2-4 Mk III)
DBB	8.6:1	195	3 Weber	Rare special series
DBC	(Special engine not produced in quantity)			
DBD	8.6:1	180	3 SU	Regular Special Series for DB2-4 Mk III
370	8.25:1	240 at 5,500	2 SU (2in)	DB4/
370/SS	9.0:1	266 at 5,750	3 SU (2in)	DB4 Vantage
370/GT	9.0:1	302 at 6,000	3 Weber	DB4 GT
and	9.7:1	314 at 6,000	3 Weber	alternatives
400	8.25:1	236 at 5,000	2 Solex	Lagonda Rapide
400	8.9:1	282 at 5,500	3 SU	DB5 and DB6
400/V	8.9:1	325 at 5,750	3 Weber	DB6 Vantage (DB5 extra)
400/S	8.9:1	282 at 5,500	3 SU	DB6 Mk 2/DBS (incl AM Vantage)
400/SVC	9.4:1	314 at 5,750	3 Weber	DB6 Mk 2/DBS (no-cost option)
400FI	9.4:1	(N/A)	AE Brico FI	DB6 Mk 2 (£300 extra) and early DBS

Chassis numbers and production records:
Aston Martin six-cylinder sports and racing cars, 1951 to 1961

Production summary

DB3	(1951-53)	10
DB3S	(1953-56)	31
DBR1	(1956-59)	4*
DBR2	(1957-58)	2
DBR3	(later converted to DBR1)	1*
DBR4	(1959-60)	4
DBR5	(1960-61)	2
TOTAL SIX-CYLINDER SPORTS-RACING ASTON MARTINS		54

(*5 DBR1s, counting DBR3/1)

DB3 — 1951 to 1953

DB3/1 — Works car; 1951 TT, fastback coupe top fitted for Le Mans 1952, then removed; supercharger tried, then removed. Last works race 1953 Thruxton. Sold Argentina.

DB3/2 — Production prototype; road-equipped works demonstration car. Raced three times in UK (1952-53) prior to sale; Barthel, UK.

DB3/3 — Works car; body rebuilt as short-tail by Chapron of Paris after 1952 Monaco crash; Vignale coupe body fitted 1953 for sale to Mike Sparken.

DB3/4 — Works car; best result 3rd in 1952 Jersey road race; later rebuilt with part-DB3S body.

DB3/5 — Works car; best results 1st in 1952 Goodwood 9hrs and 2nd in 1953 Sebring 12hrs; one-off coupe body made for Nigel Mann 1954, top later removed; now in USA, the only DB3 raced regularly in recent times.

DB3/6 — Private car; first raced on Isle of Man by Bob Dickson 1953; later lost identity, with Jaguar engine and saloon body; history further complicated by fitting of DBR2 body and DB3S engine in mid-'Sixties.

DB3/7 — Private car with special one-off fixed-head coupe body for Tom Meyer; first race Spa 24hrs, 1953; raced in 1955 club events by Angela Brown, daughter of David Brown.

DB3/8 — Private car, first raced 1953 by Ken Downing and loaned once to Reg Parnell; raced by Sir Jeremy Boles and Don Beauman in 1954.

DB3/9 — Private car, first raced 1953 BRDC Silverstone by Tony Gaze, who crashed at Oporto shortly afterwards, destroying car.

DB3/10 — Private car, first raced by Graham Whitehead 1953, then by Tony Everard 1954.

DB3S — 1953 to 1956

DB3S/1 — Works car 1953-54; winner first time (Charterhall 1953); best 1954 result, 1st Silverstone. Later owners included Roy Salvadori and Graham Whitehead; successful again a decade later when owned by Rupert Glydon.

DB3S/2 — Works car 1953-54; best result 1st in 1953 Goodwood 9hrs; sold to Peter Collins for 1955; successful club car in late-'Fifties, driven by Tom Kyffin, John Dalton and Roy Bloxam; now in Forshaw collection.

DB3S/3 — Works car 1953-54; later owners (prior to write-off) included Tony Everard and Patsy Burt.

DB3S/4 — Works car, 1953-54; best result 1st in 1953 TT; later owners included Graham Whitehead; subsequently to New Zealand.

DB3S/5 — Production car 1953, then works car 1954-56 with some good wins; often seen at AMOC meetings in recent years (C. R. C. Aston and I. Hilton).

DB3S/6 and DB3S/7 — Works cars with fastback bodies (attractive, but aerodynamically suspect), crashed by 'B. Bira' and Jimmy Stewart, respectively, at Le Mans 1954; both rebuilt as disc-braked open cars for 1955 and 1956 works seasons; both raced privately in 1957-58 by Whitehead half-brothers; both active in recent times (G. Parker and R. Pilkington, respectively).

DB3S/8 — Works car 1955-56; 1st at Spa and Oulton Park 1955; rebodied in 'Sixties, abroad; later in UK ('Seventies), Roger Hart and Bob Roberts.

DB3S/9 — Works car 1956 and early 1957; best results 1st Oulton Park 1956 and 2nd Le Mans 1956; sold to David McKay, successful in late 1957 and 1958.

DB3S/10 — Works car 1956-57 (wishbone front suspension for 1957); raced in 1958 by John Dalton and subsequently

	by private owners; one major rebuild.
DB3S/11	Works car, never raced by works. Sold to USA, eventually burnt out (1965) and rebuilt there by George Newell.
DB3S/101	Private car first raced by Ken Wharton at Oulton Park 1955; then Berwyn Baxter 1955-57; Bill Moss 1958; Gray and Agnes Mickel 1959; various subsequent owners; now in Forshaw collection.
DB3S/102 DB3S/103 and DB3S/104	Three private cars for the Australian Kangaroo Stable finishing 2nd, 4th and 3rd, respectively, in 1955 Hyères 12hrs; '102' took Australian land speed record in 1957 before sale; '103' was kept by Tom Sulman until 1961; '104' was sold to the USA and stayed there.
DB3S/105	Private car first raced by Whitehead half-brothers at Hyères 1955; special Panelcraft coupe body fitted 1956; car later sold to Hong Kong, but history gets pretty fudged thereafter.
DB3S/106	Private car for the Far East driver Chan Lye Choon; very successful from 1957-60 (Chan's best win 1958 Macau GP); car won 1961 Singapore GP (Barnwell) prior to 1963 crash in Malaya.
DB3S/107	Private car sold into Venezuela.
DB3S/108	Private car sold in UK; no real successes; later acquired by Bill Lake.
DB3S/109	(NOT USED).
DB3S/110	Private car purchased in recent times by Nigel Dawes.
DB3S/111	Private car; club racer in early 'Sixties; later to Forshaw collection.
DB3S/112	Private car raced quite successfully by former Allard campaigner Michael Graham in Western USA; later acquired Chevrolet V8 engine and, assisted by a crash, lost its original identity.
DB3S/113	Private road car (with fixed head and other visual differences from normal) for Max Aitken; later owned by Maurice Baring (1957) prior to export to USA; featured in *Road & Track* magazine.
DB3S/114	Private car raced only a couple of times by American Commander Arthur Bryant before he was killed in 1956 British Empire Trophy race at Oulton Park. Engine later used for Tojeiro-Aston Martin.
DB3S/115	Private road car USA.
DB3S/116	Private car for J. Arthur Rank organization as one of the stars of the film *Checkpoint*. Later lived an active club racing and sprinting life, mainly in Scotland (T. J. Henderson).
DB3S/117	Private car, first registered in Morocco 1956 for J. Kerguen, who won his class with French journalist Jean-Paul Colas at Le Mans 1957 (11th overall).

	Concours car in USA since the 'Sixties; George Newell's throughout the 'Seventies.
DB3S/118	Private car, raced in 1956 in UK and Benelux countries by Hans Davids (after accident, surviving parts of body thought to have been transferred to DB3S/8).
DB3S/119	Private car most recently with Nigel Dawes collection.
DB3S/120	Third production DB3S fixed-head coupe (see *Motor*, June 13, 1956); raced by Jean Bloxam (Salmon) 1958; rebuilt 1965 and owned for many years by Mr Monk.
(DB3S)	(Single-seater; raced by Reg Parnell New Zealand 1956.)

DBR 1, 2, 3, 4, and 5 — 1956 to 1960

DBR1/1	Works car for 1956 Le Mans, 2.5-litre engine; same unit used for early 1957 meetings at Oulton Park and Goodwood; then 2nd at Spa and Aintree and other 1957 races with 3-litre engine; continued as works car until 1959 when it won Nurburgring 1000kms race; crashed in private ownership 1965; protracted rebuild.
DBR1/2	Works car on its first race, Spa 1957, as 3-litre; won 1958 TT, 1959 Le Mans and TT, clinching Aston Martin's World Sports Car Championship; Major Ian Baillie owned it 1960-62, then David Ham 1963-66; later club use.
DBR1/3	Works car, won Nurburgring 1000kms 1958; burned at Goodwood 1959; rebuilt and sold to Border Reivers (Ian Scott-Watson's team) and came 3rd at Le Mans 1960; three wins in Scotland in 1961; sold to Charles Sgonina (owner of several previous Aston Martins) and owned and sprinted by him until 1966; continued club life.
DBR1/4	Works car, formerly DBR3/1, 2nd at Le Mans and 4th in TT in 1959; later in museum (Beaulieu) prior to sale in 1975 and rebuild (Peter Brewer); raced in early 'Eighties as 2.5-litre by Bill Symons.
DBR1/5	Private car for the Whiteheads, new in 1959; best result 1960 Rouen GP (Fairman, 1st); sold to South Africa and later rebuilt by Howard Cohen.
DBR2/1	Works 3.7-litre, 1957 Le Mans and Silverstone races; 3.9-litre engine for 1958 (victories at Goodwood and Oulton Park by Moss); 4.2-litre engine for George Constantine (very successful in USA and Bahamas, 1958-59); occasional UK club race appearances; then many years as road car with special body from DB3/6 (R. H. Dennis); later fitted with old body and exported to USA.
DBR2/2	Works 3.7-litre, 1957 Silverstone winner; 3.9-litre engine for 1958; 4.2-litre engine for Bob Oker, USA

DBR3/1, DBR4/1, DBR4/2 entries (left column) and DBR4/3, DBR4/4, DBR5/1, DBR5/2 entries (right column):

	1958 and 1959 (also driven by Stirling Moss in 1959 Bahamas speed week); fairly successful club racer in UK (early 'Sixties); subsequent complete rebuild.
DBR3/1	Works car using short-stroke, 3-litre version of Marek engine. Retired in only race (BRDC Silverstone, 1958) before becoming a DBR1 for 1959. *(See DBR1/4).*
DBR4/1	Works 2.5-litre GP car, 2nd at debut (Silverstone 1959) and took part in three more GP races; chassis sold (1960) to Lex Davison as spare for DBR4/4.
DBR4/2	Works 2.5-litre GP car, 1959-60, unsuccessful; chassis scrapped in 1961.
DBR4/3	Works 2.5-litre revised GP car, late 1959 and 1960, unsuccessful; sold late 1960 to Bib Stilwell; raced in New Zealand and Australia 1961-63; regular club performer in UK (Peter Brewer) throughout late 'Sixties; now in Donington collection.
DBR4/4	Private 1960 GP car with 3-litre engine, owned by Lex Davison and raced by him in Australia and UK (1960-62); successful historic racer from 1968 (Neil Corner).
DBR5/1 and DBR5/2	Works lightweight 1960 GP cars; unsuccessful; chassis scrapped in 1961.

APPENDIX G
Aston Martin six-cylinder racing engine development

Model/type	Bore × Stroke	cc	BHP at RPM	Carburation	Cylinder head	First raced
DB2	78 × 90mm	2,580	116 at 5,000	2 SU H4	60° cast iron	Le Mans 1949
DB2	78 × 90mm	2,580	128 at 5,000	2 SU H4	60° alloy*	Silverstone May 1951
DB2	78 × 90mm	2,580	138 at 5,500	3 Weber 35DCO	60° cast iron*	Le Mans 1951
DB3	78 × 90mm	2,580	133 at 5,500	3 Weber 35DCO	60° alloy*	Dundrod 1951
DB3	83 × 90mm	2,922	147 at 5,000	3 Weber 36DCF	60° cast iron	Monaco 1952
DB3S	83 × 90mm	2,922	182 at 5,500	3 Weber 35DCO	60° cast iron	Charterhall May 1953
DB3S	83 × 90mm	2,922	225 at 6,000	3 Weber 45DCO	60° alloy 12-plug	Silverstone May 1954
DB3S	84 × 90mm	2,992	240 at 6,000	3 Weber 45DCO	60° alloy 12-plug	Dundrod 1955
DBR1	83 × 76.8mm	2,493	212 at 7,000	3 Weber 45DCO	60° alloy 12-plug*	Le Mans 1956
DBR1	83 × 90mm	2,922	240 at 6,250	3 Weber 45DCO	60° alloy 12-plug	Spa May 1957
DBR1	83 × 90mm	2,922	252 at 6,000	3 Weber 45DCO	95° alloy 12-plug*	Spa August 1957
DBR1	84 × 80mm	2,992	242 at 6,000	3 Weber 45DCO	95° alloy 12-plug	Goodwood (TT) 1958
DBR2	92 × 92mm	3,670	287 at 5,750	6 Weber 48DOE	80° alloy	Le Mans 1957
DBR2	95 × 92mm	3,910	284 at 5,500	3 Weber 50DCO	80° alloy	Goodwood April 1968
DBR3	92 × 75mm	2,992	258 at 7,000	6 Weber 48DOE	80° alloy 12-plug	Silverstone May 1958
DBR4	83 × 76.8mm	2,493	250 at 7,800	3 Weber 50DCO	95° alloy 12-plug	Silverstone May 1959
DBR5	83 × 76.8mm	2,493	245 at 7,500	Lucas PI	80° alloy 12-plug	Silverstone May 1960
DP212	96 × 92mm	3,995	327 at 6,000	3 Weber 50DCO	80° alloy 12-plug	Le Mans 1962
DP214	93 × 92mm	3,740	317 at 6,000	3 Weber 50DCO	80° alloy 12-plug	Le Mans 1963
DP215	96 × 92mm	3,995	326 at 5,800	3 Weber 50DCO	80° alloy 12-plug	Le Mans 1963
DP212	98 × 92mm	4,164	349 at 6,000	3 Weber 50DCO	80° alloy 12-plug	(see below)

Notes:
* Alloy cylinder heads were used experimentally in 1951, but they were not successful. Cast iron was the regular material until the new alloy head (two plugs per cylinder) appeared at the May 1954 Silverstone meeting.
* The DB2 was raced as a 2.9, developing some 150bhp, in the 1953 Mille Miglia and several other events.
* Experimental short-stroke 2.5 engine was first raced in a DB3S in April 1956 at Oulton Park.
* The wide-angle cylinder head (95° between inlet and exhaust valves) and dry-sump lubrication made the 2.9 and 3.0 DBR1 cars' engines lose much of their original 'LB6' identity from 1957.
* The 4.2 engine was first used in the two DBR2 cars, sent to the USA in 1958 (not being eligible for World Sports Car Championship events); later they also received 12-plug heads. The final entry (for DP212, above) refers to the specification when the car was sold at the end of 1963.

Six-cylinder Aston Martin and Lagonda performance figures

Type	Lagonda 2½ dhc	Lagonda 2½ sal	DB2	DB2	DB2	DB2	DB2-4(2.6)
Chassis No	UMD 266	UMC 382	LML/50/7	LML/50/9	LML/50/10	LML/50/9	LML/50/221
Reg No	105bhp	105bhp	VMF 63	VMF 65	VMF 37	VMF 65	YMP 200
Quoted power	*Motor*	*Autocar*	116bhp	105bhp	105bhp	105bhp	125bhp
Source	14.9.49	11.11.49	*Motor*	*Autocar*	*Motor Sport*	*Autosport*	*Autocar*
Date	90.2	91	27.9.50	17.11.50	Feb 51	2.3.51	2.10.53
Mean maximum speed (mph)			116.4	110	109	110	111
Acceleration (sec)	5.4	5.6					
0-30mph	9.1	—	4.1	5.1	5.0	—	4.4
0-40mph	12.9	12.3	5.8	—	6.0	—	—
0-50mph	17.6	18.2	8.6	9.9	9.6	8.2	8.9
0-60mph	24.9	25.5	11.2	12.4	12.7	10.8	12.6
0-70mph	39.2	42.2	14.9	17.1	15.8	—	17.2
0-80mph	—	—	19.0	21.1	20.7	—	22.5
0-90mph	—	—	25.1	27.2	29.8	—	31.2
0-100mph	21.7	—	34.5	38.8	—	35.4	40.4
Standing ¼-mile (sec)	17.0	18-20	18.5	—	—	—	18.9
Overall fuel consumption (mpg)	—	—	20	—	—	—	20.3
Typical fuel consumption (mpg)			—	17-20	18	20-24	20-22

Type	DB2-4 (2.9)	DB2-4(2.9)	Lagonda 3L sal	DB2-4 (Mk II)	DB2-4 (Mk II)	DB Mk III	DB Mk III
Chassis No	LML/669	LML/669	167 GMC	AM 300/1145	AM 300/1145	AM 300/JB/1401	
Reg No	4 AML	4 AML		4 JHX	4 JHX	147 MMC	98 MMG
Quoted power	140bhp	140bhp	*Motor*	140bhp	140bhp	162bhp	195bhp
Source	*Motor*	*Autocar*	19.12.56	*Autocourse*	*Autosport*	*Autocar*	*Autocourse*
Date	25.8.54	3.9.54	104	May 57	31.5.57	27.12.57	Jan 59
Mean maximum speed (mph)	118.5	118.7		119.2	118.4	119	124*
Acceleration (sec)			3.8				
0-30mph	4.2	3.8	6.3	3.6	3.5	3.5	3.2
0-40mph	6.0	—	9.1	5.2	—	—	4.8
0-50mph	8.2	8.1	12.9	7.8	7.2	7.1	6.4
0-60mph	10.5	11.1	16.8	10.0	10.0	9.3	8.2
0-70mph	13.8	14.8	23.8	13.2	—	13.1	11.6
0-80mph	17.7	18.6	33.9	16.4	17.2	16.7	14.8
0-90mph	22.2	23.7	—	20.6	—	22.3	18.2
0-100mph	30.0	31.7	19.5	27.0	28.0	31.0	23.8
Standing ¼-mile (sec)	17.9	17.9	14.5	—	17.0	17.4	—
Overall fuel consumption (mpg)	23.0	20.1	—	—	23	18.1	—
Typical fuel consumption (mpg)	—	18-22		20-25	—	16-22	—

Type	DB4	DB4	DB4GT*	DB4GT Zagato†	DB4 Vantage	DB5	DB5
Chassis No	DB4/257/R	DB4/776/R	0167/R	0184/R	DB4/1011/R	1451/R	1725/R
Reg No	4 XMD	7851 MM	40 MT	4359 ML	432 FLD	DMM 5A	DKX 10B
Quoted power	240bhp	240bhp	302bhp	314bhp	266bhp	282bhp	282bhp
Source	Motor	Autocar	Autosport	Autocar	Car & Driver	Autocar	Motor
Date	14.9.60	13.10.61	8.12.61	13.4.62	July 63	18.9.64	6.2.65
Mean maximum speed (mph)	139.3	140.6	152.5	152.3		141.3	145.2
Acceleration (sec)							
0-30mph	4.3	3.5	2.4	2.8	2.6	3.4	3.1
0-40mph	5.7	4.9	—	3.6	3.8	4.4	4.2
0-50mph	7.2	6.7	4.6	4.8	4.8	6.4	5.6
0-60mph	9.3	8.5	6.4	6.1	6.8	8.1	7.1
0-70mph	11.4	10.6	—	8.0	8.5	10.8	8.8
0-80mph	13.6	12.5	10.2	9.5	11.0	13.2	11.2
0-90mph	16.7	17.7	—	12.0	13.7	16.0	13.7
0-100mph	20.1	21.7	14.2	14.1	16.8	20.1	16.9
Standing ¼-mile (sec)	16.8	16.1	14.0	14.5	15.4	16.0	15.4
Overall fuel consumption (mpg)	16.5	16.4	14.4	13.9	—	14.7	17.6
Typical fuel consumption (mpg)	17.7	14-19	—	12-19	14-22	12-21	19.3

Type	DB6	DB6	DB6	DBS	DBS
Chassis No	2353/R	2353/R	2546/R	5102/R	5102/R
Reg No	LBH 8C	LBH 8C	NPP 5D	EPP 8G	EPP 8G
Quoted power	325bhp	325bhp	325bhp	325bhp	325bhp
Source	Motor	Autocar	Autosport	Autocar	Motor
Date	8.1.66	25.2.66	21.10.66	10.10.68	21.12.68
Mean maximum speed (mph)	147.6	148	152	140	141.5
Acceleration (sec)					
0-30mph	2.6	2.6	2.6	3.4	—
0-40mph	3.7	3.6	—	4.6	3.8
0-50mph	4.9	5.1	4.8	6.7	5.6
0-60mph	6.1	6.5	6.0	8.6	7.1
0-70mph	7.4	8.2	—	10.5	9.2
0-80mph	9.9	10.7	9.8	13.5	12.2
0-90mph	12.3	13.2	—	16.2	14.7
0-100mph	15.0	16.0	14.9	19.6	18.0
Standing ¼-mile (sec)	14.9	14.5	14.9	16.3	15.3
Overall fuel consumption (mpg)	12.5	12.6	—	12.7	10.9
Typical fuel consumption (mpg)	14.6	12-18	12-15	13.0	14.1

Notes:
* Works experimental lightweight
† Zagato body
The DB6 and DBS test cars were to Vantage specification